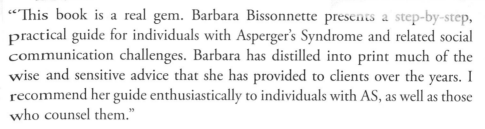

"'This book is a real gem. Barbara Bissonnette presents a step-by-step, practical guide for individuals with Asperger's Syndrome and related social communication challenges. Barbara has distilled into print much of the wise and sensitive advice that she has provided to clients over the years. I recommend her guide enthusiastically to individuals with AS, as well as those who counsel them."

—*Teresa Bolick, PhD, BCBA-D, licensed psychologist, author, and speaker*

"In today's times, no one can guarantee employment but Barbara Bissonnette's book provides thorough instruction to young spectrum adults. Her readers will be well-prepared and ahead of many others when those employment opportunities arise."

—*Michael John Carley, Executive Director, GRASP and author of* Asperger's from the Inside-Out: A Supportive and Practical Guide for Anyone with Asperger's Syndrome

"Barbara Bissonnette has written the book we have all been waiting for—one to help college students on the spectrum with the post-graduation employment search. Bissonnette presents strategies for students with AS to comprehend the very social, non-verbal world of interviews and colleague interactions. She gives us sample emails, conversation starters, forms, and detailed checklists— just what we need to increase the percentage of employed people on the spectrum. Plain talk about the interview process, translation of interview questions, and how to negotiate this difficult phase of the job search will be this book's gift to the reader. Thank you Barbara!"

—*Jane Thierfeld Brown, EdD, Co-Director, College Autism Spectrum and Assistant Clinical Professor, Yale Child Study*

"In my experience Barbara Bissonnette is a unique individual. She is a neurotypical who really—and I mean really—understands Asperger's Syndrome. Her ability to talk the spectrumite language whilst retaining the objectivity of a dispassionate observer enables her to provide genuine, incisive expertise, and support as a specialist career development coach in the field of Asperger's Syndrome."

—*Malcolm Johnson, author of* Managing with Asperger Syndrome

"From determining career options, locating positions, presentation of self in media, written form, and interviews, to appropriate disclosure, this book is packed to the brim with suggestions, tips, worksheets, lists, and just plain old great advice. While perfectly tuned to those with Asperger's Syndrome searching for employment, this book will be helpful to anyone looking for a job."

—Stephen Shore, EdD, Professor of Special Education, Adelphi University, and internationally renowned author, consultant, and presenter on issues related to the autism spectrum

"Barbara Bissonnette has a unique understanding and vast experience with working with individuals with Asperger's Syndrome in employment. Her book is a critical asset for career counselors, teachers, and parents assisting young adults to obtain and keep employment taking into account the environmental, sensory, and social fit for each individual. This is a must read and I highly recommend it."

—Michael P. McManmon, EdD, founder of the College Internship Program and author of Made for Good Purpose: What Every Parent Needs to Know to Help Their Adolescent with Asperger's, High Functioning Autism or a Learning Difference Become an Independent Adult

"Although she is not herself on the spectrum, Barbara Bissonnette has demonstrated that she understands the challenges that autism brings. *The Complete Guide to Getting a Job for People with Asperger's Syndrome* addresses key job-hunting concerns that spectrumites have, from interviewing and personal presentation, to building confidence, maintaining motivation, and managing anxiety. The book is a great addition to the other career guides for those on the spectrum already out there, and builds on what has come before."

—Yvona Fast, Support Groups Manager, GRASP, and author of Employment for Individuals with Asperger Syndrome or Non-Verbal Learning Disability: Stories and Strategies

The Complete Guide to Getting a Job for People with Asperger's Syndrome

of related interest

Business for Aspies
42 Best Practices for Using Asperger Syndrome Traits at Work Successfully
Ashley Stanford
ISBN 978 1 84905 845 2
eISBN 978 0 85700 501 4

Employment for Individuals with Asperger Syndrome or Non-Verbal Learning Disability
Stories and Strategies
Yvona Fast
ISBN 978 1 84310 766 8
eISBN 978 1 84642 015 3

How to Find Work that Works for People with Asperger Syndrome
The Ultimate Guide for Getting People with Asperger Syndrome into the Workplace (and keeping them there!)
Gail Hawkins
ISBN 978 1 84310 151 2

Asperger Syndrome Employment Workbook
An Employment Workbook for Adults with Asperger Syndrome
Roger N Meyer
Foreword by Tony Attwood
ISBN 978 1 85302 796 3
eISBN 978 1 84642 989 7

Managing with Asperger Syndrome
Malcolm Johnson
ISBN 978 1 84310 199 4
eISBN 978 1 84642 029 0

A Self-Determined Future with Asperger Syndrome
Solution Focused Approaches
E. Veronica Bliss and Genevieve Edmonds
Foreword by Bill O'Connell
ISBN 978 1 84310 513 8
eISBN 978 1 84642 685 8

THE COMPLETE GUIDE TO GETTING A JOB FOR PEOPLE WITH ASPERGER'S SYNDROME

Find the Right Career and Get Hired

BARBARA BISSONNETTE

Jessica Kingsley *Publishers*
London and Philadelphia

First published in 2013
by Jessica Kingsley Publishers
116 Pentonville Road
London N1 9JB, UK
and
400 Market Street, Suite 400
Philadelphia, PA 19106, USA

www.jkp.com

Library of Congress Cataloging in Publication Data
A CIP catalog record for this book is available from the Library of Congress

British Library Cataloguing in Publication Data
A CIP catalogue record for this book is available from the British Library

ISBN 978 1 84905 921 3
eISBN 978 0 85700 692 9

Printed and bound in the United States

To my husband, Michael, in gratitude for his love, encouragement, and unflagging support.

To the men and women with Asperger's Syndrome who I have the privilege to know. I see how hard you work, and I know what you have to offer. Change is coming, and change is slow. Do not give up.

And to my mentor and dear friend, Ellen Korin. Couldn't have done it without you. Thanks.

CONTENTS

CHAPTER 1

WHY IS IT SO MUCH WORK TO GET A JOB?

On the corner of my desk is a book called *The Very Quick Job Search, Get a Better Job in Half the Time!* (Farr 2004). It has over 500 pages and weighs in at two pounds. I like this book and recommend it frequently. Still, I smile at the irony. *A quick job search in 500 pages?!*

Clearly, there is a lot to know about finding work.

Since 2006, I have provided career development coaching to individuals with Asperger's Syndrome. There is even more for them to know. I am haunted by the words of one coaching client, who has Asperger's Syndrome and has earned a Master's degree. She had been looking for a job in her field of study for more than two years. "People tell me that I am 'high functioning,'" she said, "but what good is being high functioning if I can't find a job?"

Finding employment isn't easy for people on the autism spectrum. One often-quoted statistic is that 85 percent of autistic adults are either un- or under-employed. A recent study published in *Pediatrics* found that nearly 35 percent of young adults with autism did not have paid employment, or additional education or training, years after leaving high school (Cooper *et al.* 2012). I do not know of any statistics about the employment rate for adults with Asperger's Syndrome. But it is clear that even those individuals who have four-year and advanced college degrees face significant challenges finding and retaining employment.

There is no shortage of advice for job seekers. My internet search on "how to find a job" yielded 119 million results. Amazon lists thousands of books on the subject.

Yet, if you have Asperger's Syndrome, you probably find much of the advice confusing, overwhelming, and sometimes, downright dumb. If you are searching for your first job, you may be confused about what kind of work you will like and be able to do. If you have lost a job—or several—in one field, you may have no idea of what would be a better match. Perhaps your current job is very stressful, or not very challenging, and you want to find a different one but aren't sure how.

You may have read that most people find their jobs through networking, but can't imagine ever walking into a room full of strangers to ask for work. Shouldn't earning a degree or completing a vocational training program be enough to get hired?

If you are like my clients, the process itself may seem fraught with contradictions and rituals that don't make sense. Joe couldn't understand why it was okay to apply for a job that required two years of experience, when he had only been working for 19 months. Michael wondered why he would be expected to discuss previous jobs during interviews, since they were listed on his resume. Valerie worried that it was conceited to talk about her strengths and accomplishments. Jim didn't know why he shouldn't tell an interviewer that his weaknesses are low self-confidence and procrastinating when they specifically ask.

If some or all of the above sounds familiar to you, you are not alone. Your questions, concerns and confusion have nothing to do with your intelligence, your qualifications, desire to work, or effort to find a job. They are due to fundamental differences in the way that your brain and a neurotypical (NT) brain processes information. If you haven't heard the term before, *neurotypical* refers to a person who is not on the autism spectrum. There is nothing inherently wrong with the way that your brain operates. It is just different from how the NT brain works. However, people with NT brains (often called neurotypicals) make up the majority of the population, and make the hiring decisions in organizations. In order to find a job, you need to communicate your abilities in a way that neurotypicals understand.

In many ways, conducting a job search is like adapting to a foreign culture. In order to fit in, you need to understand certain rules and expectations. Employers evaluate job candidates based on their education, experience, and skills. The decision about who to hire is largely driven by how well an individual will be able to work with other people in the organization.

The purpose of this book is to demystify the job search process, and help you find work that is both satisfying and manageable. It is designed to present a roadmap to employment, beginning with identifying suitable work and ending with a job that matches your abilities.

ROADMAP TO EMPLOYMENT, CHAPTER BY CHAPTER

1. In the remainder of this chapter, I will share some observations about how Asperger's Syndrome impacts employment, and common barriers to finding work. There are also notes about how to use the information in this book.

2. In Chapter 2, the journey begins with an exploration of your interests, talents, and skills. You will identify work criteria that are important to you, and describe your ideal work environment. I will ask you to look at the ways that Asperger's Syndrome impacts you, and explain how to use that information to avoid jobs that will be difficult or impossible to manage. You will also develop a list of potential jobs to research.

3. By the end of Chapter 3, you will have narrowed down your list of occupations to those that seem like the best matches. I will show you how to conduct preliminary research using several different resources. The emphasis will be on understanding how well a particular job matches your skills, education, and other important criteria. You will be asked to describe the positive and negative aspects of each occupation you research, and then rate your level of interest.

   You will also learn *exactly* how to conduct an informational interview. This is when you talk to someone who is already working at the job you are interested in, so that you can learn more about it. The process is described in detail: how to find people to meet, how to set up an interview, what to say when you arrive, the kind of questions to ask, and how to end the meeting. There's a bonus: the skills you learn in this chapter will be used again during networking and job interviewing.

   Job shadowing and strategic volunteering will also be explained.

4. The way that you present yourself to a potential employer sends messages about the kind of employee you will be. In Chapter 4, you will learn about the ways that you are communicating nonverbally throughout the job search process. You will discover how to avoid sending unintended messages, and how to manage the way that others perceive you.

5. Finding a job means marketing yourself to employers. Chapter 5 explains why this process is not to be feared. You will get step-by-step

instruction on creating a resume that generates interviews. You will also learn how to avoid mistakes that will land your resume in the "no" pile.

Applying for jobs that you are not qualified for wastes time and energy. I will explain how to decode the language of job posts, so that you understand the primary tasks, required versus negotiable skills and experience, and the work environment.

Finally, I'll describe how to write a convincing cover letter.

6. Chapter 6 focuses on another aspect of successfully marketing yourself: developing a realistic job search plan. A variety of job search strategies will be reviewed, including networking. You will learn three ways to network if you're not socially savvy, and how to create a search plan that gets results.

7. Interviewing is a complex social event and a challenge for nearly everyone with Asperger's Syndrome. Chapter 7 explains how interviewers evaluate candidates, how to prepare answers to traditional and behavioral interview questions, how to research a company, and what questions to ask the interviewer. Negotiating salary and managing job references are also addressed.

8. Whether or not to disclose a disability to an employer is a personal decision. Chapter 8 describes how laws, like the Americans with Disabilities Act, protect individuals with disabilities in the workplace. You will understand the pros and cons of disclosing at each phase of the job search. This chapter also includes examples of accommodations, and a process for requesting them in a strategic manner.

9. Looking for a job is stressful, and usually a long-term process. You have to accept a lot of "nos" before you get a "yes." Chapter 9 offers suggestions for setting realistic goals, maintaining motivation, and managing anxiety.

10. Finally, in Chapter 10, I will share some concluding thoughts about how to put the information in this book to use for your own job search.

COMMON BARRIERS TO EMPLOYMENT

Before I started my coaching practice, I worked in business and held positions where I made hiring decisions and managed staff. As a coach, my clients have ranged in age from 15 to 63. Those who are entering the job market usually need assistance to figure out the right type of job, write a resume, learn interviewing skills, and create a job search plan. Others seek me out when they want to make a career change, have lost a job, or need to address challenges in their current workplace.

Nearly all of my clients are seeking competitive employment. This means that they are competing in the labor force like everyone else. Their jobs range from entry-level positions to managerial and professional occupations that pay six-figure salaries. Specific jobs include: technical writer, creative writer, editor, production manager, graphic artist, fine artist, teacher (toddlers to graduate students), physicist, supply chain manager, project manager, sales manager, consultant, computer programmer and other IT professional, engineer, analyst, actuary, accountant, lawyer, paralegal, administrative assistant, retail sales associate, warehouse worker, electrician, physician, nurse, librarian, library clerk, meteorologist…and more!

Every individual is unique. However, I am able to make some general observations concerning Asperger's Syndrome and employment based on patterns I have observed in my coaching practice.

- Interest in a subject doesn't necessarily mean that you will enjoy, or be able to make a living in, that field.

- A college degree does not guarantee employment.

- Work environment can be as or even more important than specific tasks for employment success.

- Employers are more willing to overlook "eccentricities" if you have skills that are in demand, or are exceptional in your job performance.

- Job candidates are evaluated on their education, skills, experience, and perceived ability to fit in. Fitting in is usually most important.

- Just because a job is entry-level doesn't mean that it is manageable for someone with Asperger's Syndrome. There may be demands for multitasking, speed, or interpersonal communication that you cannot handle.

Adam is like many job seekers I coach: frustrated and discouraged. He graduated near the top of his class with a degree in computer science. With some help from his father, Adam put together a resume, drafted a cover letter, and began applying for software testing jobs posted on internet job boards. After sending more than 40 resumes, Adam received an invitation for a telephone interview. Confident about his technical ability, Adam anticipated no problems answering questions.

The interview did not go as planned. Adam hadn't kept a copy of the job advertisement, and had a hard time answering specific queries about his qualifications. Since he hadn't done any research on the company, he wasn't prepared to explain why he wanted to work there. When asked about whether he had experience using a specific tool, Adam responded, "No," even though he was proficient with one that was very similar (and could have called attention to this). The call lasted ten minutes.

Rather than change his job search strategy and the way that he prepared for interviews, Adam simply continued to visit job boards twice a week. He knew that he had skills that were in demand, yet his resume wasn't working. He refused to consider any type of networking. As the weeks became months, Adam spent less and less time looking for work.

There is a lot of truth to the expression that finding work is a full-time job. It doesn't mean that you have to literally spend eight hours per day, Monday through Friday, trying to find a job. But you *do* need to make a substantial commitment of time and effort. As one client said, "It used to be that you had to be expert in your work; these days you need to be expert at finding a job."

At this writing in mid-2012, the global economy remains volatile and weak. The unemployment rate in many countries is high. The decline of some industries has forced people to change careers because there are not enough jobs in their previous line of work. Even in fields that are growing, it is taking longer to find work.

It is also true that jobs *are* available and people *do* get hired. Those who have an effective plan and take consistent action almost always find work faster than those who don't have a plan. I have observed certain patterns among individuals who have been looking for more than eight months. Do any of these apply to you? If the answer is yes, don't worry. Each point will be addressed in this book!

1. *Seeking work in a highly competitive field.* There are certain industries that attract many more qualified candidates than there are job openings,

such as the performing arts, law, and broadcasting. Other fields are so specialized that there are a very limited number of opportunities, for instance, astronomy, and museum management. Economic downturns, the introduction of a new technology, or a regulatory change can make some jobs scarce or obsolete. Opportunities may also be limited by your geographic region—there will be many more chances for a broadcasting career in New York City, for example, than in rural Ohio.

It is a personal decision to look for a job in a very competitive field. Some people are willing to engage in a protracted search. They may take "survival jobs" in order to pay their bills. However, if employment is your primary goal, you may need to choose an occupation in a growing field.

2. *Applying for jobs when you don't know if you are qualified.* Although you do not need to meet 100 percent of the criteria in a job post, you do need the critical competencies and experience. Joe assumed that because he had a degree in communications, he was qualified for jobs in broadcasting, multimedia, social media, marketing, and editorial. He read job titles, not job descriptions, and applied for many positions for which he lacked basic qualifications. Our first order of business was to determine what jobs Joe was qualified to do.

3. *Seeking too many different jobs.* Kevin's search included writer, web developer, tutor, and customer service representative. He believed that this range increased his odds of getting hired *somewhere*. In practice, this strategy made it difficult for him to locate opportunities and adequately prepare for interviews. Additionally, Kevin's last web development job was four years ago, and his skills were out of date. His resume was a patchwork of disparate jobs.

4. *Unrealistic expectations.* I've had a number of clients tell me that they do not want to start at the bottom of a profession, or that they will only consider a certain salary, without knowing whether it matches what employers will pay. Others believe that a very high IQ or a 4.0 grade point average (GPA) is enough to get them hired. Careful career research enables you to set realistic expectations.

5. *A resume that isn't generating interviews.* Your resume is a marketing document. Its purpose is to clearly communicate your qualifications, so

that you will be invited for an interview. An effective resume highlights skills, experience, and accomplishments that are relevant to the job that you are seeking *now*. It must also be easy to read and free of errors. Kevin's resume stated that he was detail oriented, yet contained three typographical errors!

6. *Not working while you look for a job.* There are several benefits to doing some kind of work, even if you are not paid for it, while you are looking for your desired job. It provides current experience for your resume, and possibly, some income. The people you work with might have job leads. Having something to focus on beside a job search provides structure to the week and helps to keep your spirits up.

7. *Responding too slowly to opportunities.* Clients sometimes show me job posts that are several weeks old, wanting to know whether they should apply. It is very likely that after two weeks, the interviewees have been selected, and the interviewing process has begun. It is important that you apply to new openings in a timely manner.

8. *"Winging it" on job interviews.* A cursory read through a book or website about how to answer interview questions is not adequate preparation. Clients frequently tell me that they forget how to answer questions, or get caught up on basic inquiries, such as, "Why do you want to work here?" Practicing interviewing skills should be part of your weekly job search plan. If you *think* an interview went okay, that you *probably* answered questions well, or *can't remember* what you were asked, you need more practice interviewing.

9. *Finding a job is not a priority.* A sure way to know that this applies to you is if you have "upside down days." That is, you stay up very late indulging a hobby, such as playing computer games, then sleep late the next morning. Kevin told me about a call he received at 11:00am in response to his resume. He asked the interviewer if he could call her back because, "I just got up." Kevin was surprised when she didn't respond to his message, but I wasn't. Would you be enthusiastic about a job candidate who sleeps until 11:00am?

    If you are serious about employment, you must treat your search like a job. Starting your day no later than 9:00am is good discipline. If you are currently employed and looking for another job then schedule specific, non-work times during the week to devote to your search.

10. *Your job search plan consists only of sending resumes to posted openings.* It cannot be stressed enough that passively sending resumes through the internet is the hardest way to find work! According to *The Very Quick Job Search*, only about 15 percent of job openings are advertised. Those that are tend to be low-paying, high-turnover jobs, or specialized positions requiring skills that are hard to find (Farr 2004, p.13).

    This does not mean that you should not visit job boards or apply to openings. However, it significantly increases your chances of an interview if you network with people in your field of interest.

HOW TO USE THIS BOOK

This book is designed to show you how to compete in a job market dominated by neurotypicals. This does not mean changing who you are or lying about your capabilities. You will learn how to determine jobs you are able to do, and communicate how you fill an employer's need.

Throughout the book, I will explain the "whys" behind aspects of the job search that many people with Asperger's Syndrome find confusing or silly. I'll use examples from my coaching of clients to illustrate various points. Names and identifying details have been changed, and, in many cases, composites have been used to protect people's privacy.

There are many specific skills used in a job search. It takes time and practice to master new skills. Some of my clients become very frustrated if they cannot write a resume, call someone on the telephone, or answer an interview question perfectly the first time. They get discouraged and decide that they cannot do the task, period. The problem isn't that they *can't*. They haven't learned the skills and practiced enough.

A job search also involves a lot of different activities. If you begin to feel overwhelmed, take a break. Focus on one aspect at a time. If one step is too big, break it down into smaller steps. If you are stuck, ask for help.

I have observed an interesting phenomenon among individuals with Asperger's Syndrome. Although they are very generous and eager to help other people, they resist requesting help for themselves. Everyone needs assistance from time to time. If you are having difficulty, the smart thing to do is find someone knowledgeable who can offer advice or information. This could be a family member, mentor, therapist, or coach.

The focus of this book is on professional jobs that require a resume and sophisticated interviewing skills. However, if the work you are seeking involves filling out applications on site, for example at a restaurant or retail store, you will still benefit from much of the information. Understanding how to improve your personal presentation, greet an interviewer, and communicate your abilities is important for *any* job.

As you go through the steps of clarifying your abilities and important criteria, researching occupations, and speaking to people who are already employed in a field, you might change your mind about what job you want. This is not unusual. A college degree is not "wasted" if you don't work in your field of study. In a lot of cases, it is not necessary to earn another degree to move to a different line of work.

If you have already tried several different jobs without success, the job search process outlined in this book is particularly important. It will help you to understand whether you need to learn or improve certain skills, or retrain for a different line of work.

Many chapters contain templates related to aspects of the job search. These templates are marked with a tick and readers have permission to download them for their personal use, from www.jkp.com/9781849059213/resources.

CHAPTER 2

FINDING THE RIGHT JOB OR CAREER

Vocational success depends on a variety of factors. These include:

- interest in a particular field

- possessing the necessary talents, skills, and education

- availability of jobs

- opportunities for advancement

- being valued for one's contribution.

For individuals with Asperger's Syndrome, additional factors include:

- very clear performance expectations

- limited interruptions during the day

- being able to finish one task before starting another

- getting answers to detailed questions

- concrete, step-by-step instructions

- an explanation of the big picture

- manageable levels of interpersonal interaction.

The right job match is about much more than being interested in a topic. In this chapter and the next one, you will learn how to match information about your interests and abilities with the requirements of an occupation. Don't skip over or rush through these activities. The better the match between your attributes and preferences and the job requirements, the greater your chances of success.

Choosing the right occupation is like fitting together pieces of a puzzle. Ideally, you will find work that: is related to your interests, emphasizes your talents and skills, meets most of your important work criteria, and minimizes your limitations. When I work with clients, we go through these areas one by one.

There is a template at the end of this chapter that will enable you to create your Ideal Employment Profile.

MATCHING INTERESTS TO OCCUPATIONS

If you are like many people with Asperger's Syndrome, there is at least one subject in which you are passionately interested. Indulging this interest brings you happiness and relaxation, and you probably know a *lot* about this interest.

There are individuals with Asperger's Syndrome who are able to create rewarding careers based on their special interests. One of my clients, with a passion for numbers, is a Certified Public Accountant; another, who is fascinated by computers, is a software programmer.

Identifying interests is one piece of the employment puzzle. However, it is a mistake to assume that because you are interested in a certain subject, you will enjoy and be able to make a living working in that field. The problem with this assumption is that you may not be suited for the available jobs.

It is true that many neurotypicals choose college majors or vocational training without thinking about the nature of the jobs that await them. The difference is that neurotypicals are more easily able to adapt to a variety of different tasks and work environments. This is not true for people with Asperger's Syndrome.

The first question that I ask clients about their interests is, "What do you envision yourself doing once you are employed as [fill in the blank]?" The answer I hear most often is, "I don't know. I haven't thought about it."

This is a critical question to answer. Otherwise, you might invest a lot of time, energy, and money pursing the wrong occupation. Rick was looking for a career related to his passion for baseball. "What I want," he explained, "is a quiet, low stress, behind-the-scenes job."

Initially, Rick's idea of a "behind-the-scenes" job was managing team travel for a major league baseball club. He based this choice on one detail: it would involve working in an office rather than amid the chaos of screaming fans in a stadium. Once he understood the primary job tasks, and the skills needed to complete them, Rick made a realization. Managing team travel is a high-pressure job that requires a degree of multitasking that he simply couldn't handle.

The first step is to create a list of possible occupations, based on your interests. You may have very definite ideas about jobs that you want to pursue. Or, you may not be sure of how your interests could translate into employment. Perhaps you have tried unsuccessfully to work in one field, and want to find a better match.

A Word about Assessments

There are a variety of career assessments that measure interests, aptitudes, behavioral style, personality type, leadership ability, values, and more.

My opinion is that these assessments are of limited value for people with Asperger's Syndrome, because they have been developed by and for neurotypical people. The results assume average or better interpersonal communication skills and executive functioning. The career suggestions do not consider deficits in understanding the perspective of others, extreme sensitivity to sensory stimulus, slow processing speed, and other common challenges. No test can predict with certainty *anyone's* occupational success. However, if you have Asperger's Syndrome, be aware that you need to thoroughly investigate an occupation and its requirements to determine if it is right for you.

Although it is not a career tool, I believe that an up-to-date neuropsychological evaluation can provide valuable information for career planning. Widely used in the diagnosis of Asperger's Syndrome, it measures cognitive abilities in areas such as attention, memory, language, visual-spatial abilities, and executive functioning. The results can be helpful in choosing occupations that maximize strengths, and minimize areas of weakness.

For example, someone with poor working (short-term) memory will have trouble in jobs that require significant multitasking, or the ability to remember long sequences of verbal instructions. An individual with auditory processing problems may need significant accommodations to function in noisy environments, or in a job with lots of group interaction. For the person with poor visual-spatial abilities, a career in architecture is unlikely.

These evaluations are usually performed by a clinical neuropsy-chologist, who includes vocational recommendations.

Even if you feel certain about your vocational choice, I encourage you to complete a career interest inventory. These assessments suggest possible careers based on topics and activities that appeal to you. They do not measure whether you have the aptitude or skills to succeed at an occupation. They suggest several different vocational possibilities.

There are many career interest inventories. Some are administered through career professionals. Others are available to the general public online. There are free assessments and others that require a fee. The Occupational Information Network (O*NET) offers the O*NET® Interest Profiler™ (www.onetcenter. org/IP.html). The Riley Guide (www.rileyguide.com), a comprehensive source of employment information, lists many self-assessment tools in the "Before Your Search" section of its website.

Whether you take an interest assessment, or do other vocational research, you should have a list of between four and ten occupations of interest. The next chapter explains how to narrow down these choices by conducting thorough career research. For now, your focus is on developing a list of possibilities.

IDENTIFY YOUR TALENTS AND SKILLS

For as long as Jim could remember, he'd had a passionate interest in professional sports. Other people were amazed at his recall of facts about individual players and statistics about the performance of various teams. His college major was sports management, and he began his job search immediately after graduation.

Entry-level event management and marketing positions were not attractive to Jim because of the rapid pace and high degree of multitasking. There were few jobs in journalism and broadcasting. He had no interest in the manufacturing or retail selling of sporting equipment. Jobs requiring math skills, such as a statistician, were out of the question. Jim read that sales positions were the usual point of entry for management careers. After more than a dozen interviews, he had not received any job offers.

Jim was confused and discouraged and began coaching to find out what was going wrong. When we met, one problem was immediately apparent. Jim spoke in a monotone and showed almost no facial expression. Two of the important criteria for sales people are energy and enthusiasm. Jim's body language and voice projected neither. Job ads described ideal candidates as confident, dynamic, competitive, and driven. "That's not really who I am," he said.

I work with a lot of people, like Jim, who decide on an occupation without fully understanding what they do well, and what skills they want to use on the job.

Suppose that your interest is video games. Jobs in this field include game designer, programmer, animator, audio engineer, writer, tester, technical support specialist, public relations manager, and positions in marketing and sales. Each job requires different aptitudes and abilities. Animators must have artistic talent along with skills using graphic design software programs. Programmers need analytic ability and skills in software engineering or computer programming.

The second piece of the occupational puzzle is identifying your talents and skills. These terms are often used interchangeably, although they are different. Talents are natural abilities; skills are learned.

One way to identify your talents is to think back to what came easily to you when you were a child. Were you drawn to mathematics or science? Did you enjoy writing, drawing, building things, or observing the world around you? Did you have an ear for music, a flair for acting, or abilities in sports or dance?

If you are having a hard time pinpointing your talents, you may want to explore the work of psychologist John Holland. He identified six work environments that correspond to six different personality types. "Holland's Theory" is that a person will be most satisfied in a work environment that matches his personality. The six styles are realistic, investigative, artistic, social, enterprising, and conventional. The Self-directed Search is an assessment that measures your Holland type, and suggests possible careers that match. It is available online for a modest fee at www.self-directed-search.com.

Skills are abilities that are learned and developed over time. No one is born knowing how to use a computer program or wire a building for electricity. A person needs various skill sets in order to carry out the tasks that make up his job. Job skills are categorized as "hard" and "soft." Hard skills refer to technical proficiency and soft skills relate to interpersonal interaction.

Many hard skills are transferable, meaning that they are used in a variety of occupations. Effective written communication is an example of a transferable hard skill. The ability to exchange information in emails, letters, reports, or other documents is required for many different jobs. Problem solving is another example. Nearly every job requires the ability to assess a situation, review options, and decide a course of action.

Hard skills can also be specific to a particular job. Drawing blood, operating a cash register, preparing income tax returns, or using HyperText Markup Language (HTML) to develop a website are job-specific skills.

Soft skills (also known as people skills) are the most troublesome for people with Asperger's Syndrome. Skills in this area relate to interpersonal communication and the ability to work with others. They are hard to quantify (what, exactly, is good collaboration?), and are abstract concepts that can be difficult to learn. Neurotypicals place a high value on soft skills in the workplace.

Some occupations require much more sophisticated levels of communication and interaction than others. The higher one's rank in an organization, the greater the emphasis on relationships with other people. Managing a staff and leading a team require well-developed soft skills. Later chapters of this book will explain how to gauge these requirements and your ability to meet them. For now, be aware that soft skills include the ability to listen, negotiate, and persuade as well as personal characteristics, such as persistence, honesty, loyalty, detail orientation, and helpfulness.

Occupations that emphasize your primary abilities will be easier to manage and more satisfying. I have had a number of clients who struggle, sometimes for years, in jobs that emphasize their areas of difficulty. When you know what you do well, you can look for work that utilizes those capabilities. You might also discover that there are specific hard and soft skills you need to acquire in order to qualify for your desired job.

The Ideal Employment Profile template at the end of this chapter includes lists of hard and soft skills.

THE IDEAL WORK ENVIRONMENT AND IMPORTANT JOB CRITERIA

It is my experience that the work environment can be as important as, or even more important than, job tasks for individuals with Asperger's Syndrome. You might excel at the technical aspects of your work, but have difficulty prioritizing tasks, meeting deadlines, dealing with interruptions, working quickly enough, or communicating with colleagues. Erin's technical documentation was high quality, however, she could not write quickly enough to meet deadlines. Bill lost an administrative position because he kept forgetting the procedure for processing documents.

My clients have been remarkably consistent in describing the environments that are most conducive to their success. Characteristics include:

- being able to finish one task before beginning another

- minimal interruptions during the day, and a limited amount of multitasking

- a relaxed pace without urgent deadlines or pressure to work quickly

- knowing what to expect each day

- explicit direction on the scope of a project, priorities, and tasks that need to be done

- quantifiable performance expectations

- supportive supervisor and co-workers

- a quiet workspace that is free of strong odors, bright lights, and loud sounds

- the right level of interpersonal interaction.

I have never had a client say to me that he wanted to work alone all day. Instead, people tell me that they want time by themselves to concentrate on projects, and also some interaction with their co-workers. Determining the right level of interpersonal interaction for you is an important consideration. It varies by person. You may need to spend the majority of the workday focused on your own projects. You might enjoy communicating with people in your department, but become anxious about interfacing with co-workers you don't know in other parts of the company. Servicing customers could be manageable in controlled, tightly scripted situations, but not in those requiring quick decision-making.

There are also practical considerations that can influence your satisfaction. Important criteria can be the length of your commute to and from work, not having to work overtime, or choosing work in a field that is growing and offers many job options. You might need a job that is very structured, or prefer work that is more creative. You may need to work part time, or find a job with flexible hours.

In addition to establishing your important criteria, you need to decide where you are willing to compromise. No job will match your ideal 100 percent. Compromise is about prioritizing, and differentiating essential elements from personal preferences. Initially, Carl was concerned about accepting a data entry position because the commute meant that he would not be able to eat dinner at the customary 6:00pm. On further reflection, he agreed to compromise and change his dinner schedule in order to secure employment.

Compromising in the short term can lead to greater benefit in the long term. A person might accept a lower salary in order to break into a field, or establish themselves in a particular company. Doing work that one is not passionate about, but that provides steady income and a pleasant environment, might lead to greater personal happiness.

The Ideal Employment Profile includes questions to help you determine your best working environment and important work criteria.

UNDERSTANDING PERSONAL LIMITATIONS HELPS YOU MAKE BETTER CAREER DECISIONS

Every human being has limitations of one kind or another. Some of my clients are concerned that admitting weaknesses means that they are "less than" others or that they cannot be successful. My experience is the opposite. I have found that the more an individual understands about how Asperger's Syndrome impacts him, the easier it is to find and sustain employment. He is able to choose jobs that minimize his areas of challenge.

I place limitations into two categories. There are those that can be mitigated by learning new skills or utilizing assistive technology. There are also challenges that a person can't do much to change. I look at these limitations as signs that point that person away from occupations that would be difficult or impossible to manage.

Eric had a limitation from the first category. He wanted a job doing website design. However, he did not have proficiency using HTML or cascading style sheets (CSS), two basic competencies for this work. Once he acquired these skills, the limitation was gone.

For many of my clients, interviewing is a "category one" limitation. At first, it seems confusing and intimidating. But once they learn what the questions really mean, and how to communicate their abilities, they are able to practice and build their confidence. The job offer follows.

Slow brain-processing speed is a category two limitation. Processing speed cannot be changed. A job that requires taking in information from several sources simultaneously, analyzing it, and making a quick decision would be very difficult for someone with slow information processing. Similarly, a person who has poor working (short-term) memory will not do well at a job that requires rapid attention-shifting.

The final section of the Ideal Employment Profile lists the common challenges faced by Asperger's individuals, and asks you to rate their impact. I encourage you to make an honest assessment of your limitations. You can also ask someone you trust, and who knows you well, to rate you and then compare their responses with yours. Remember, some personal limitations can be changed and others have workarounds. Your strengths help to offset your limitations.

PERFORMING A SWOT ANALYSIS

Another tool that you can use to profile your abilities and limitations is a SWOT analysis.

SWOT is an acronym that stands for Strengths, Weaknesses, Opportunities, and Threats. It is used frequently in business for strategic planning. You can perform your own personal SWOT analysis as part of your employment planning.

In addition to your own assessment, you can ask people who know you for their evaluation. These can be family members, a friend, mentor, coach, or other professional. Comparing your responses with those of others can provide a clearer picture of your situation.

The four SWOT questions are as follows.

1. *What are your strengths?* These include personal attributes plus resources that give you an advantage. List the following:

   a) Things that you do well, such as talents and specific skills.

   b) Personal characteristics, such as honesty, persistence, and intelligence.

   c) Education, which can include formal degrees or vocational training, as well as certificates, continuing education workshops, and internships.

   d) People you know who can help you reach your career goals. This can include current and former co-workers, college professors or alumni, and family members.

e) Other resources, such as having the time and money to return to school, or access to specialized equipment.

2. *What are your weaknesses?* This encompasses personal limitations as well as external factors that can slow or derail your employment search. List the following:

   a) Personal difficulties, such as organizing time, remembering appointments, multitasking, managing anger, anxiety, etc.

   b) Job-related skills that you need to acquire or improve. These can be hard skills, such as learning computer applications, as well as soft skills, like being punctual, interviewing, interacting with co-workers, or asking for help.

   c) External factors, such as multiple job losses, no references, a large gap in employment, work experience that doesn't match education (e.g. Master's degree, but employed as retail sales associate), limited mobility (e.g. no access to public transportation).

   d) Unrealistic expectations about your qualifications, salary, or the effort required to find a job.

3. *What are your opportunities?* These are the positive potentials available to you. Describe the following:

   a) Industry trends or regulatory changes you can capitalize on. The weak economy has created a demand for bankruptcy attorneys; the "green movement" is creating jobs in fields like sustainable energy.

   b) Growth industries where you can transfer your skills, or qualify for state- or employer-sponsored training.

4. *What threats do you face?* List the obstacles that are getting in the way of your employment goal, such as:

   a) Weaknesses or unrealistic expectations from question 2 that you must to address to be employable.

   b) External factors, such as new technology, that are making jobs obsolete, or seeking employment in a highly competitive field with few job openings.

A SWOT analysis enables you to identify opportunities that you haven't considered, and areas that you need to address to maximize your chances for success. There is a SWOT analysis template at the end of this chapter.

SELF-EMPLOYMENT

After losing several jobs, Melissa decided to capitalize on her writing and editing skills by becoming a freelance writer. Her plan was to produce technical marketing materials for specialized segments of the healthcare industry.

Self-employment was attractive to Melissa for a number of reasons:

- She could work alone on her assignments, without distraction, from home.

- Interaction with others was limited, which was less stressful and reduced the chances of committing a social *faux pas*.

- The quality of her work was more important than her interaction with others.

- There were no office politics.

- Assignments consisted of specific tasks (writing and editing) that were her strengths.

- She could work at her own pace.

The last point was especially important to Melissa. The quality of her work was high, but she lost jobs because she couldn't meet deadlines. Melissa was willing to base her rates on the amount of time it would take a neurotypical to complete assignments. This way, she would be competitive. "If I have to work a few extra hours and not charge for them," Melissa explained, "it will be worth it."

There were also challenges.

Melissa had to market her services. This involved identifying potential client companies and the individuals who would hire her. She needed to describe the benefits of her services in a compelling way. She had to plan various marketing activities, meet with people, and ask for business. Potential clients asked her to submit proposals and price quotes.

Starting her business required an investment in an up-to-date computer, high-speed internet connection, stationery, website, and other items. Melissa had to prepare invoices and keep track of payments. She paid an accountant to figure out her quarterly income tax payments.

As a business owner, Melissa paid for her own health insurance and did not get any paid vacation time or sick days. Her income varied each week. During her first year in business, Melissa had to use a portion of her savings to augment her earnings.

Even though Melissa was in charge of her company, she had to accept direction from her clients. Since they were paying for the service, *they* set the scope and budget. Clients expected that Melissa would meet prearranged deadlines. If she didn't, they wouldn't hire her again. This sometimes meant that Melissa had to work on weekends and holidays. She also had to accept feedback diplomatically, and at times, compromise her ideals in order to keep a client satisfied.

This is not to discourage you from self-employment. The ability to set your own work hours, perform specific tasks, and work at your own pace makes this an attractive option for some people. If you find a niche and supply services that are in demand, it can be lucrative.

You do need to understand that running your own business involves more than providing the service or making the product. You need to budget your time, meet deadlines, handle administrative duties, and interact with prospects and customers. If you are not willing or able to sell your product or service, you can hire someone to handle this task, but obviously this will lower your income.

I know of individuals with Asperger's Syndrome who run successful businesses, some on a part-time basis, performing personal services: dog walking, lawn mowing, and house cleaning. Others provide professional services: marketing, writing, bookkeeping, accounting, and consulting. Others are fine artists and sell their work at galleries, over the internet, and at craft shows. A parent or spouse may help to manage the business.

Here are suggestions about how to determine if self-employment is right for you:

- Read books about how to start and grow your own business. Some enterprises can be started fairly quickly, with a minimal investment. Others require substantial investments of time and money, and may be tightly regulated. If you are thinking about offering a professional service, I highly recommend *Get Clients Now!™: A 28-Day Marketing Program for Professionals, Consultants, and Coaches* by C. J. Hayden (2006).

- Do basic market research. Find out as much as you can about your competitors, who they serve, what they charge, and what makes your enterprise different. Are there enough potential customers, who can pay what you need to charge? Can you reach them cost-efficiently?

- Get some advice from experts. The U.S. Small Business Administration (www.sba.gov) website has information and resources covering every aspect of starting and growing a business. Readers in other countries can check whether there are similar government agencies. There may be a non-profit organization in your community that offers consultations and workshops. Some will critique your business plan at low or no cost. Professional association websites may have information about self-employment opportunities.

- Talk to potential customers. Describe your idea and listen to their feedback. This will help you to discover whether there is a need for what you offer, and what people would be willing to pay.

- Review your finances. It can take several months to several years to establish a business. Do you have enough savings to pay your expenses in the meantime? Can you work part time to earn income while you get your venture off the ground?

- Honestly assess your readiness to have your own business. How willing, and able, are you to market your product or service? Will you be able to budget your time effectively to manage all of the different aspects? What is your tolerance for ambiguity, especially regarding weekly income?

Self-employment is not for everyone. If your motive for starting a business is to avoid going on job interviews, not have a boss, or not to have to interact with others, think again. You will have to convince customers to hire you, keep them happy, and communicate effectively with them.

✓

IDEAL EMPLOYMENT PROFILE

YOUR INTERESTS, TALENTS, AND SKILLS

1. What are your interests?

   _____

   _____

   _____

2. What jobs and careers are you most interested in (list up to ten)?

   _____

   _____

   _____

3. Circle your job-related talents and skills in the list below. This list is not exhaustive, so feel free to add additional items.

Acting	Estimating	Organizing
Advising	Evaluating (a process, someone's performance)	Persuading
Analyzing (data, situations)		Photographing
		Presenting
Assembling	Examining (a patient, information)	Proofreading
Budgeting		Public speaking
Building		Reasoning
Calculating	Explaining	Recording information
Caring for animals	Handling complaints	
Caring for people		Repairing
	Influencing	

Caring for things (plants, artwork, records)

Categorizing

Classifying

Compiling

Composing music

Coordinating (events, people's work)

Counseling

Creating

Decorating

Deciding

Demonstrating

Designing

Drawing

Editing

Initiating

Innovating

Inspecting

Interpreting (data, languages, terminology)

Inventing

Investigating

Leading

Listening

Meeting deadlines

Meeting the public

Monitoring

Motivating

Negotiating

Observing

Operating (equipment)

Researching

Scheduling

Selling

Summarizing

Supervising

Teaching (children, adults, animals)

Testing

Troubleshooting

Updating

Visualizing (a process, object, outcome)

Writing (business, technical, creative, instructional)

Additional skills:

_____

_____

4. Review the items you circled, and write down the ten talents and skills you most enjoy using:

_____

_____

_____

✓

5. Circle your most important personal characteristics from the list below. Feel free to add additional items.

Accurate	Energetic	Orderly
Adaptable	Enthusiastic	Organized
Analytical	Flexible	Outgoing
Assertive	Focused	Patient
Big picture thinker	Follow instructions	Persistent
Careful	Friendly	Practical
Concrete	Hardworking	Precise
Confident	Helpful	Punctual
Conscientious	Honest	Quick learner
Creative	Imaginative	Reliable
Curious	Independent	Responsible
Decisive	Intelligent	Sense of humor
Dependable	Logical	Systematic
Detail oriented	Loyal	Take initiative
Determined	Methodical	Thorough
Efficient	Motivated	Trustworthy

Additional skills:

_____

_____

6. List your job-specific skills here (e.g. CSS and HTML, word processing software, programming, or foreign languages):

_____

_____

_____

IMPORTANT CRITERIA AND IDEAL WORK ENVIRONMENT

1. How many hours do you want to work per week?

   _____

2. What is your maximum commute (time and distance)?

   _____

3. How will you get to and from work (drive an automobile, use public transportation, walk)?

   _____

4. How much money do you need to make?

   _____

5. How much money do you *want* to make?

   _____

6. Are you willing/able to obtain further training in order to qualify for a particular job?

   _____

7. Do you prefer to perform the same duties every day, different duties every day, or a combination of both?

   _____

8. Do you need a job that is very structured, where you know exactly what you need to do, or one that allows you to decide what tasks to do and when?

   _____

9. Do you need a job with a slow and steady pace?

   _____

10. Can you manage at a job with tight deadlines and surprise projects?

    _____

✓

11. How do you prefer to work?

   ☐ Alone for most of the day.

   ☐ Minimal interaction with co-workers.

   ☐ Lots of interaction with co-workers.

   ☐ Interaction with people inside and outside of the organization.

12. What kind of supervision do you need?

   ☐ Close, including contact with my supervisor several times per day.

   ☐ Daily check-ins.

   ☐ Minimal supervision (e.g. weekly).

   ☐ Prefer to be self-employed.

13. Do you want to work indoors or outdoors?

_____

14. Do you prefer an environment that is formal or informal?

_____

15. Are you better at analytic, linear problem solving or intuitive, big picture thinking?

_____

16. Do you prefer detailed, well-defined work or creative/strategic work?

_____

17. Which of the following do you prefer working with?

   ☐ Facts and information

   ☐ Numbers

   ☐ Ideas

   ☐ Your hands

☐ People

☐ Animals

18. Check the characteristics that are very important for you to have in a job:

☐ Challenges my intellect

☐ Involves some risk

☐ Includes travel

☐ Utilizes my creativity

☐ Helps others

☐ Allows me to express my ideas

☐ Work that I like

☐ Lots of opportunity for advancement

☐ Good benefits

☐ Lots of vacation time

☐ Being needed

☐ Job security

☐ Low stress

☐ Low responsibility

19. What other criteria are important to you?

_____

_____

_____

_____

_____

PERSONAL LIMITATIONS

1. Rate any challenge areas that apply to you. A rating of mild/moderate means that the limitation is a problem sometimes. A rating of serious means that it is a problem most of the time. You can also ask someone who knows you well to fill out this section, and compare the rating they give to yours.

✓

Challenge Area	Mild/Moderate	Serious
Making adequate eye contact		
Blurt out my thoughts (unintentionally offend/anger others)		
Interrupt		
Uncomfortable meeting new people (what to say/how to act)		
Speak too loudly/softly/rapidly/monotone		
Hard to follow group conversations		
Take words literally and misunderstand instructions/expectations		
Slow to process verbal information (prefer written material)		
Easily distracted		
Not sure how to start projects/what the steps are		
Black and white thinking (hard to see options)		
Work too slowly		
Difficulty prioritizing		
Difficulty multitasking (rapid attention-shifting)		
Hard to refocus if interrupted during a task		
Act impulsively, based on too little information		

Managing time (scheduling tasks, knowing how long they should/will take, arriving on time, meeting deadlines)		
Controlling frustration/anger (yell, shut down, walk away, cry)		
Anxiety (especially meeting new people, learning new task)		
Dual-track processing (e.g. writing while listening, looking at someone and listening)		
Other:		
Other:		
Other:		

2. Describe the type of work environment and tasks that would be very difficult for you to manage (e.g. noisy, many interruptions during day, little supervision, lots of multi-step tasks, etc.):

_____

_____

_____

✓

SWOT ANALYSIS

SWOT stands for Strengths, Weaknesses, Opportunities, and Threats. Complete the four questions below. You can also ask people who know you well for their evaluation.

1. *What are your strengths?* These include personal attributes plus resources that give you an advantage.

    a) Talents and skills:

    _____

    _____

    _____

    b) Personal characteristics:

    _____

    _____

    _____

    c) Education (formal, internships, certificates, workshops):

    _____

    _____

    _____

    d) People who can assist you:

    _____

    _____

    _____

e) Other resources:

_____

_____

_____

2. *What are your weaknesses?* This encompasses personal limitations as well as external factors that can slow or derail your employment search.

a) Personal difficulties:

_____

_____

_____

b) Missing or inadequate skills or knowledge:

_____

_____

_____

c) External factors:

_____

_____

_____

d) Unrealistic expectations:

_____

_____

_____

✓

3. *What are your opportunities?* These are the positive potentials available to you.

   a) Industry trends or regulatory changes to capitalize on:

   _____

   _____

   _____

   b) Growth industries in need of my skills:

   _____

   _____

   _____

4. *What threats do you face?* List the obstacles that are getting in the way of your employment goal.

   a) Weaknesses or unrealistic expectations from question 2 that must be addressed:

   _____

   _____

   _____

   b) External factors:

   _____

   _____

   _____

CHAPTER 3

RESEARCHING OCCUPATIONS

Now that you have completed your Ideal Employment Profile and SWOT Analysis, and have compiled a list of jobs that interest you, the next step is to conduct occupational research.

The importance of thoroughly researching occupations cannot be overstated. Job titles are not reliable indicators of tasks and responsibilities. The more you know about the primary tasks, required skills, and working conditions, the better your chances of choosing work that you can manage. You should also research various industries to understand the working conditions.

Sharon hadn't considered that veterinarians, in addition to diagnosing and treating sick animals, also interact with pet owners, sometimes under very stressful, emotional circumstances. She also learned that many are self-employed, and work long hours and on weekends. The pace, interpersonal interaction, and 60-hour-plus workweek prompted her to explore other, less stressful, jobs that involve working with animals.

Do You Already Know What You Want to Do?

Even if you already know what job you want, don't skip occupational research. You might discover jobs that you hadn't considered, that pay more, are less stressful, or are otherwise a better choice. The research will also help you to write a better resume and prepare stronger answers to interview questions. Don't skip it!

Steven's story illustrates the importance of thorough research. Within days of graduation, he began looking for a job in government, figuring that his major in political science, interest in research, and 3.8 GPA would result in multiple offers. Instead, he discovered a highly competitive field where employers expected applicants to have internships or related volunteer experience on their resumes.

Many of the entry-level jobs required administrative skills that Steven lacked. The greatest concentration of positions was in the Washington, D.C. area, and Steven did not want to move across the country. Eleven months later, he wasn't thinking about shaping public policy. His priority (and that of his parents) was *any* job that would provide steady income.

Perhaps you have been in the workforce for a while, and are struggling in a profession that demands too much interpersonal communication or organizational ability. A fear of change, inability to see options, or inaccurate assumptions can lock people into high-stress jobs they can barely manage, or result in repeated job losses.

For Ed, a decade in the legal profession left him exhausted and frustrated. After graduating *cum laude* from law school, he passed the bar exam on his first try and became an attorney at a small law firm. He was asked to resign after a few months, and quickly found work at another law office. Two years later, he was fired from this job, and then went on to hold four more positions that ended in his being fired or asked to resign. In total, Ed had six different jobs over the course of ten years.

Initially, Ed's intention was to find yet another attorney job. A review of his career history revealed some telling patterns. During his tenure at each firm, Ed did not socialize with his fellow attorneys, preferring to eat lunch by himself every day. His abrupt manner and refusal to follow office rules that he thought were "stupid" alienated him from the administrative personnel. The life-long discomfort Ed felt in social situations kept him from attending professional events where he was expected to make new contacts.

As he described each job, a greater and greater fatigue seemed to engulf Ed. "Do you like practicing law?" I asked. "No," he admitted, "My father wanted me to be a lawyer. My love is research, but I can't afford to go back to college." We began exploring how Ed could transfer his legal expertise into a research-oriented occupation.

GETTING STARTED WITH PRELIMINARY RESEARCH

Online occupational databases are excellent sources of preliminary data. The Occupational Outlook Handbook (www.bls.gov/ooh) and O*NET (www.onetonline.org) are two such sites in the United States. They can be accessed at no charge. If you live outside the United States, search online for "occupational information" to find resources in your country.

These databases describe all kinds of different jobs. Descriptions include information about tasks and responsibilities, work environment, types of employers, educational requirements, and employment outlook. You can learn what type of skills are required (both hard and soft), average wages, and whether advanced degrees or certifications are recommended. As importantly, the work environment is described in terms of typical hours, pace of the job, equipment used, and level of stress.

Links to related careers reveal allied occupations that might be a better match for your abilities, require less training, or offer more employment opportunities in your geographic region.

Here is what you can learn from an occupational description. You probably think of a customer service representative as someone who assists customers who have questions or problems. The job seems pretty straightforward: listen to the customer's need, and provide a solution. But is it really that simple?

The following description of customer service representative is from the Occupational Outlook Handbook, which is produced by the United States Bureau of Labor Statistics. This is an excerpt of the full description, which I have edited in places. The numeric keys correspond to my comments, which are at the end of each section. This style is used throughout the book to explain examples.

Sample Occupational Description:
Customer Service Representative

When the customer has an account with the company, a representative will usually open the customer's file in the company's computer system. Representatives use this information to solve problems and may make changes to customer accounts, such as to update an address on file or cancel an order.❶ They also have access to responses for the most commonly asked questions and to specific guidelines for dealing with requests or complaints.❷

Some workers specialize in a particular mode of communication, such as voice, email, or chat, but others communicate with customers through more than one contact channel. For example, voice agents, who primarily deal with customers over the phone, may respond to email questions when there is downtime between calls.❸

[Job tasks can vary.] For instance, representatives who work in banks may answer customers' questions about their accounts, whereas representatives who work for utility and communication companies may help customers with service problems, such as outages.❹

Representatives who work in retail stores often handle returns and help customers find items in their stores.❺ Some representatives may help to generate sales leads, sometimes making outbound calls in addition to answering inbound ones, although selling is not their main job.❻

(Source: Bureau of Labor Statistics, U.S. Department of Labor, Occupational Outlook Handbook, 2012–13)

My observations about the nature of the work are as follows.

❶ The job requires the ability to access a computerized customer database.

❷ You must follow the company's instructions on how to answer questions and resolve problems. You may encounter unexpected situations.

❸ The job may require dual-track processing, such as speaking with a customer on the telephone while simultaneously typing their responses into a database.

❹ The job may require specific technical training.

❺ Retail settings involve a lot of face-to-face contact with customers.

❻ Generating or qualifying sales leads involves asking questions and possibly describing products or services.

Work Environment

Customer contact center workers usually sit at a workstation with a telephone, headset, and computer. These centers may be crowded and noisy, and the work can be repetitive or stressful, with little time between calls.❶

Companies usually keep statistics on customer service representatives to make sure they are working efficiently. This helps them keep up with their call volume and ensure that customers do not have to wait on hold for a long time.❷

Because many call or customer contact centers are open extended hours or are staffed around the clock, these positions may require workers to take on early morning, evening, or late-night shifts. Weekend or holiday work is also common. In retail stores, customer service representatives may have to work evenings and weekends as these are peak times for customer traffic in stores.❸

(Source: Bureau of Labor Statistics, U.S. Department of Labor, Occupational Outlook Handbook, 2012–13)

My observations about the work environment are as follows.

➊ A large call center environment may not be acceptable if you are sensitive to noise, or become anxious when there are a lot of people around you. Expect to be at your station except for scheduled breaks.

➋ There is pressure to resolve calls quickly. Some individuals may be anxious knowing that their efficiency is being monitored.

➌ You will need to be flexible with your work hours, and be willing to work evenings and on holidays.

Important Qualities

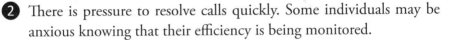

Communication skills. Customer service representatives…must listen carefully to customers to understand their needs and concerns to be able to resolve the call as efficiently and effectively as possible.❶ Workers who interact with customers by email, live chat, or other non-voice contact channels must write well, using correct grammar, spelling, and punctuation.❷

Interpersonal skills. Customer service representatives interact with many different people. Creating and maintaining positive relationships is an essential part of a customer service representative's job.❸

Patience. Workers must be patient and polite, especially when dealing with difficult or angry customers.❹

Problem-solving skills. When addressing customer issues, customer service representatives need to analyze situations, investigate problems, and determine solutions.❺

(Source: Bureau of Labor Statistics, U.S. Department of Labor, Occupational Outlook Handbook, 2012–13)

My observations about the important qualities (which are soft skills) are as follows.

1 The job requires strong listening and problem-solving skills. You may need to probe for information or ask clarifying questions. The solution you offer will be based on correctly evaluating the customer's situation and on the company's policies.

2 Written communication must be well organized and make the point quickly. This requires the ability to organize, prioritize and summarize information. You must be able to produce written communication with enough, but not too much, detail, and produce it quickly.

3 If a customer is rude or angry, you can't be rude or angry back. You must listen patiently and calmly as the customer explains the situation or vents their frustration. Being able to gauge their level of agitation helps you know what to say.

4 Even if a customer is being unreasonable or mean, *your* tone of voice must communicate understanding and a willingness to help. Responding is easier if you can put yourself into the customer's shoes. If strong emotions from other people make you anxious or upset, this job is probably not for you.

5 Investigating could involve researching customer records, product information, or getting status updates (e.g., an estimate of when cable service will be restored). Problem solving requires understanding the big picture, the options that are available and judgment in deciding which solution is best.

This sample occupational description illustrates how different from each other jobs with the title of customer service representative can be. Some involve heavy interaction with the public. Others require in-depth technical knowledge and/or specific industry experience (e.g. healthcare). Still others are quasi-sales positions that demand in-depth product knowledge and the ability to interact with customers and members of a sales team.

The Job Research Template at the end of this chapter is designed so that you can record occupational information in an organized way. Later in this chapter, you will learn about additional sources of preliminary research. You can add to the template as you learn more.

Here are some things to keep in mind as you conduct preliminary career research.

- It *is* preliminary. The purpose is to help you narrow your list of possibilities. You may decide to eliminate occupations that require skill sets you don't have or can't easily acquire. You might discover that a job doesn't pay enough or otherwise falls short of your must-have criteria.

- I ask my clients to rate occupations as they go through each step of their research. Jobs that receive an "A" rating seem very promising. Those rated "B" are attractive, but raise some concerns. The "C" possibilities are relegated to the "maybe" column for possible research at a later date. Those rated "D" are removed from the list of possibilities. As you continue to learn more, your rating of an occupation may change.

- Occupational descriptions are written for neurotypicals. They may not spell out requirements which to neurotypicals are obvious, such as: remembering and quickly performing sequential tasks, listening and writing at the same time, noticing visual detail, or managing your time independently. Additionally, if you focus on only a few of the details in the description, or the wrong ones, you may have an inaccurate picture of what a job really involves. One way to clarify the neurotypical perspective is to review your impressions with a career professional, coach, mentor, or family member.

- Do not confuse your interest in a subject with the ability to work in the field. Read the descriptions carefully, and focus on the tasks, skills used, and working conditions. Be open to exploring jobs that you hadn't previously considered.

- Do not look for a job that matches your ideal 100 percent, because it doesn't exist. If you are rapidly eliminating job after job, you are probably not compromising enough, or being too specific in your analysis of job requirements. Josh was ready to eliminate editorial work because he read that occasional overtime was required. Yet, there were many aspects of the work that were a great fit for his abilities. What are your long-range goals? Accepting lower pay, performing some tasks you don't like, or working occasional weekends is worth it to get a start in your career.

The rating scale at the end of the Job Research Template can be used to categorize jobs you want to learn more about, those you might consider later on, and which to remove from your list.

MORE SOURCES OF PRELIMINARY RESEARCH

Your initial research should not be limited to occupational databases. There are several additional sources of information that will help you to form a fuller picture of the job or career in which you are interested.

Professional Associations

These are organizations comprising individuals who work in the same field. There are associations of marketing professionals, technical documentation writers, engineers, business analysts—you name it! Some are national and others are local to a region or state. National associations may have local chapters.

Associations promote professionalism, keep members apprised of news and trends that affect their jobs, and facilitate networking. They typically sponsor regular member meetings and may offer workshops or conferences. Many associations publish newsletters, magazines, or reports that are free to members or sold for a fee. The larger groups have career centers on their websites that feature advice, training opportunities, and industry-specific job openings. Some enable members to post resumes. Directories of members are usually available, although access is often restricted to individuals who are paid members of the organization.

You can learn a lot about an industry and/or profession from an association website. Should you decide at a later date that you want to pursue work in the field, an association can be a valuable source of advice and networking contacts.

The internet makes it easy to locate professional associations. If you are interested in exploring the field of language interpretation, for example, you could search "association of interpreters," "Northeast association of interpreters," or "Chicago association of interpreters."

Review Job Posts

This gives you an idea of primary tasks and the skills and experience that employers in your area want. You can also notice whether there are many or few openings in your region, and who the most active employers are.

Read Trade or Professional Journals and Blogs

An internet search will direct you to publications you can read, which may be available online or at your library. This is another way to learn about industry trends and news. It also helps gauge your interest level in an occupation. If reading about a profession bores you, working in the field will probably bore you, too.

Search the Internet for Articles that Describe Jobs and Careers

These are often written by people working in the field, and offer additional insights, opinions, and descriptions that you can match to what you have learned from other sources. Searching "what does a [job title] do" should yield results.

STEPS FOR CONDUCTING PRELIMINARY RESEARCH

1. Make a list of the occupations that you want to learn more about. Most people research no more than three occupations at a time to avoid becoming overwhelmed.

2. Use a template, such as the one at the end of this chapter, to organize what you learn. Summarize what you discover in your own words. Note the positives as well as any concerns or drawbacks.

3. Rate your interest in each occupation based on what you learn.

4. Adjust your rating based on additional knowledge from other sources.

Most people conclude their preliminary research once they have one to three occupations that they are very interested in pursuing. The next stage is advanced research, which involves talking to people who are currently working in the field. This is known as informational interviewing.

You are strongly encouraged to conduct several informational interviews for each occupation that you are exploring. In addition to enhancing your understanding of what a job is like, you are practicing skills that you will use for networking and job interviewing. The following section describes, in detail, how to set up and conduct informational interviews.

ADVANCED CAREER RESEARCH

There is a limit to how much you can learn by reading about an occupation. To find out what a job is *really* like, you need to talk to people who are already working in the field. There are several ways to do this. In this section we will look at informational interviewing, job shadowing, and strategic volunteering. Informational interviewing is the most popular method, and the easiest to implement.

Informational Interviewing

This is *not* a job interview. You are asking questions to enhance what you have learned from your preliminary research.

Most of my clients get nervous when I mention informational interviewing. The thought of approaching people they don't know is intimidating. "I don't know anyone I could meet with," they protest, "and I wouldn't know what to say."

Once you learn how to set up a meeting and what to say, informational interviews aren't that scary. This is a low-risk activity. There is no job on the line; you are simply gathering information. Most professionals enjoy talking about what they do, and are happy to give you advice.

The benefits of informational interviewing are many. You learn what a typical workday is like, what it takes to be successful, and the type of skills and experience employers want. This is also a form of networking that could result in future job leads. Just as importantly, you get hands-on experience finding people to meet with, sending inquiries, conducting meetings, and following up—all skills that you will use for actual job interviews.

I recommend that individuals conduct at least three informational interviews for each occupation that they are considering. Although the specific experience of each person will be different, after three or more interviews patterns will emerge about the job, skills needed, and work environment. Amy conducted five informational interviews, and each person mentioned that technical documentation writing involved meeting tight deadlines.

Even though this is not a job interview, you must prepare as if it is. Your words, appearance, and actions must communicate professionalism, interest in the occupation, and appreciation of the individual's time. While it is possible to conduct informational interviews over the telephone or with video conferencing, in-person meetings are best.

There are five steps to an informational interview:

1. deciding what you want to learn

2. finding people to contact

3. requesting a meeting

4. conducting the meeting

5. following up after the informational interview.

STEP 1: DECIDING WHAT YOU WANT TO LEARN

Appropriate questions to ask are those that will help you understand job tasks and primary responsibilities, what the work environment is like, the amount and type of experience that employers seek, where the best opportunities are, and facts about the industry. You can also ask for advice about how to break into the field and about starting salaries.

You should ask questions that enhance the knowledge you already have about an occupation. Inquiring about basic information that you could easily get on your own ("What does an announcer do?"), gives the impression that you are not putting much effort into your research.

There are some questions that are not appropriate to ask during an informational interview. These relate to basic job readiness topics, such as how to work as part of a team, how to make small talk, or how to get organized. Do not ask personal questions, such as how much money someone earns. Also avoid questions and statements that make you sound desperate for work.

At the end of the meeting, you should ask whether the individual can recommend other people for you to contact. Referrals from a mutual acquaintance will almost always agree to meet with you. This is how you add to your knowledge base and build potential networking contacts.

If you ask for referrals, it is important that you follow through and make contact. People make referrals from their personal networks. View this as a favor. Asking for a favor and not following through is considered rude and unprofessional.

Informational interviews usually last about 30 minutes. You should prepare six to eight questions in advance. It is okay to write these down and bring the list with you. Here are some suggestions about questions to ask. Feel free to come up with your own queries, too.

- How did you get into this field?

- What do you like best and least about your job?

- What is the typical career track? (This refers to how people advance in their careers.)

- What kind of education is required?/Is [certain certification] really necessary?

- What is a typical day like?

- If you had it to do over again, would you choose this line of work? Why?/Why not?

- What is the best way to break into the field?

- Are there publications or associations that you recommend?

- What surprised you about this job/industry?

- What does it take to be successful?

- What are the most important skills and experience that employers want?

- What are the typical work hours?

- What kind of salary range could I expect? (Note: You are not asking the individual what his salary is, but about the range based on your experience level.)

- Do you know of other people I can talk to? May I say that you referred me?

Stealth Inquiries

These questions will give you an idea of the amount and type of interpersonal interaction and multitasking that may be involved, without asking directly.

- Do you work frequently with other people, or mostly by yourself?

- How would an introvert like this kind of work?

- How much collaboration do you have with others?

- On average, how many hours per week do you spend in meetings?

- How would you describe the pace of the job?

- Are there a lot of interruptions during the day?

- Would this work be difficult for someone who needs quiet time to focus on tasks?

Wrong Questions to Ask

These questions concern job readiness, or will make you seem desperate. Professionals want to help other professionals, not people who are desperate!

- I have no idea what kind of job I'm qualified to hold; what do you recommend?

- How can I learn to make small talk?

- How can I tell if my communication problems are because of me or other people?

- How does LinkedIn work?

- I'm willing to take any job. Are there openings in your company?

- What should I say when I'm asked about my greatest weakness?

When in doubt, check it out with someone knowledgeable who you trust!

STEP 2: FINDING PEOPLE TO CONTACT

After you figure out what questions to ask, you need to find people who can answer them knowledgably. Human resources (HR) personnel are not good candidates for informational interviews, unless you are exploring careers in HR. You want to meet with people who are employed in your occupation of interest.

You should target professionals who have enough experience to tell you what the occupation is really like. Experienced individuals will also have broader networks of potential referrals. People who are too junior (e.g. associates, assistants) will only be able to offer a limited perspective, and have fewer contacts. Generally, you want individuals who have the title of manager or director, or who function in that capacity. Very senior staff members, such as company presidents or senior vice presidents, will probably be too busy to meet with you, and may not have expertise related to the job you are inquiring about.

If you are exploring a writing career, you will look for people with the title of editor, reporter, or feature writer (not editorial assistant). If you want to know more about software programming, you will want to meet with a software developer, senior software engineer, or director of software development.

You may need to further define contacts by industry or company type. If you are specifically interested in a communications position at a non-profit, you will not learn as much by talking to a communications director at a consumer products company.

It is imperative that you find the names of specific individuals. Sending inquiries to the "head of engineering," or, "manager of customer service," or through the "contact us" link on a company's website will not get results. There are several ways to find people to contact.

The best place to start is with people you already know, such as family members, acquaintances, members of your religious organization, neighbors and professional service providers, such as your dentist. Even if these individuals don't know people in your occupation of interest, they know other people who might. Former co-workers or other business contacts, college professors, or classmates are also people to contact. All of these individuals are in what is called your "informal network."

You can make your inquiry in person, over the telephone, or via email. Let the individual know specifically what you are looking for. Here is an example of how you could approach someone you know well. Notice the conversational style.

Hi, Uncle Jack.

How are you and Aunt Rita? Everyone here is fine, and Dad says that he's going to call you next week about playing golf.

I am exploring meteorology careers in the renewable energy field. My interest is companies that are developing solar heating, solar thermal power, wind power, and hydroelectricity. Do you know anyone who might have contacts in the research and development departments of "green energy" companies like these, or at a municipal power plant?

I'm eager to get advice from a director of research, staff meteorologist, or head of engineering.

Thanks, Uncle Jack. I appreciate your help.

Tim

When contacting someone you don't know as well, such as a former co-worker or college professor, your tone will be more formal. If you haven't had contact with the individual for a while, include a brief update about your status. Here is an example:

Dear Professor Harris:

I hope that this note finds you well, and that you had a restful summer break.

I have decided to explore meteorology careers in the renewable energy field. My interest is companies that are developing solar heating, solar thermal power, wind power, and hydroelectricity. I'm eager to meet with research directors, staff meteorologists, and engineering directors to get some advice about the "green energy" field, and what positions might be a good match for my interests and skills. Can you direct me to anyone who could help?

Thank you for your help, Professor Harris. If you need additional information, call me at 617-555-5555.

Sincerely,

Tim Jones

You are not bothering people by asking for their help, nor is this nepotism. Nepotism is when you are hired or promoted because you are a relative. Most people will be flattered that you asked, and happy to assist you. They will probably remember occasions when they received help, and want to pay the kindness forward.

Finding Contacts Outside of Your Network
You may need to go outside of your existing network to find contacts for informational interviews. The internet makes it easy to find individuals who have the expertise you need.

- Trade and professional associations may post member directories on their websites (access may be limited to paid members only). The people who run the association, such as the executive director and various committee members, can be good contacts and will know many people in the industry. Check out the authors of newsletter or magazine articles or blogs, as well as speakers at association events and conferences.

- Familiarize yourself with the major professional conferences and periodicals that serve the profession or industry. Conference speakers and professionals who contribute articles may be willing to share their expertise. Try to meet in person with local individuals.

- Your local Chamber of Commerce may list member organizations. A Chamber of Commerce is an organization that promotes local businesses. The members are typically small businesses. This is also a way to familiarize yourself with employers in your area.

- The online business networking site LinkedIn (www.linkedin.com) boasts millions of users. Once you create a profile, you can begin searching the LinkedIn database to locate individuals by name, company, special interest groups, and more. The basic service is free. LinkedIn will be discussed in more detail in Chapter 6.

Here is an example of how you can use these tools to find professionals and business owners to contact for informational interviews. Josh wanted to find out more about the job of archivist. He logged onto LinkedIn, and searched the database of groups using the keyword "archivist." One of the 39 results was New England Archivists, which is also a local professional association. He visited the association's website, and found the names of archivists who volunteered on various committees.

Josh needed more information about the individuals in order to decide who he should approach for an informational interview. So he went back to LinkedIn, this time searching by people. He discovered that one of the committee volunteers works as an archivist at a local museum.

This was exciting to Josh, since he was particularly interested in archiving historical items. The museum archivist was an excellent match for his needs. Rather than sending an inquiry through LinkedIn, Josh visited the museum's website, where he not only found the archivist's contact information, but a professional biography as well.

It took about five minutes for Josh to find the name of a promising contact.

STEP 3: REQUESTING A MEETING

Imagine receiving an email from someone you don't know that says, "Hello, my name is Tim. I need some advice about becoming a meteorologist. Would you talk to me? Email me back, please." You would delete—maybe even double delete—the message. Who is Tim? Why is he contacting you? Why would you give advice to a total stranger?

Now imagine receiving an email that began, "I enjoyed your article on advances in forecasting that appeared in the fall issue of *Weather Times*. My name is Tim Jones, and I recently earned a Master's degree in applied meteorology. I am exploring careers in the renewable energy field, and would like your advice."

This inquiry is from a young person who shares your interest in meteorology and is exploring jobs in the field—just like you did when you were starting out. "How nice that he read my article," you would think. "I've been doing this work for almost 20 years, and have a lot of advice to share. I could find some time to meet with Tim next week."

The difference between these two inquiries is that the second established a connection between the sender and receiver. The opening paragraph provided enough information about Tim's background to establish that he was serious about the field. The reason for his inquiry was clearly stated. Even though the two had never met, Tim established a point of commonality by mentioning the article in the professional publication.

Asking someone to meet with you is commonly done via email or postal letter. This correspondence must immediately establish a connection between you and the other individual. If you were referred by a mutual acquaintance, say so. Other points of connection can be that you heard the person speak at an event, read their blog, or have a mutual membership in a group. The introductory paragraph should also state why you are making contact.

Once the context is established, your query should summarize, in one or two paragraphs, your background and experience. This gives the recipient an idea of how they can assist you. For example, are you a recent graduate looking for advice, or an experienced professional considering a career change?

In the closing, ask for a meeting. Use language that is decisive and assumes a positive response. Avoid hesitant requests that make you seem unsure of yourself, "If by some chance you have time to meet with me." Let the individual know that you will follow up with a telephone call. I consider it a courtesy to include your contact information, in case the individual prefers to reply to you first.

Your informational interview query should be no longer than one page. If you are using email, print out a draft to check for length. If you include your resume, make it clear that the purpose is to supply additional information about your background. You do not want to give the impression that you are looking for a job.

This is an example of an email query. A printed letter would include the date, recipient's name and title, company name and address, and the sender's address.

Dear Mr. Davis:❶

Professor Smith of ACME University suggested I contact you❷ for some advice. I recently earned a Master's degree in applied meteorology and am exploring careers in renewable energy.

My postgraduate work included quality control and statistical analysis on a large climatological database to improve convective wind forecasting techniques. In addition to learning programming languages, such as Fortran and Perl, I gained experience with statistical and meteorological software packages.

I am eager to learn about opportunities in solar heating and solar thermal power that would be a good match for my interests and skill in data visualization and meteorological analysis.❸

I would like to arrange a brief meeting in the next week or two. I will call you at the end of the week to see about your availability.❹ If it's more convenient, you can reach me at 617-555-5555 or via email at tjones@isp.com.❺

Sincerely,❻

Timothy Jones

❶ Request is addressed to a specific individual; salutation is Mr. or Ms.; colon is the correct punctuation for business correspondence.

❷ Introduction establishes a professional connection and explains the reason for making contact.

❸ Sender's qualifications and experience are briefly summarized in two paragraphs.

④ Closing requests a meeting and states follow-up action. Sender's contact information gives the recipient the option of replying first.

⑤ Sender uses a professional email address.

⑥ If this were a printed letter, you would leave four spaces between the closing and your name for your signature (in blue or black ink).

Establishing a Connection

These are examples of how to establish a connection when you do not have a referral from a mutual acquaintance.

1. You read an article or blog post that the individual authored:

   Dear Mr. Smith:

   I enjoyed your article on advances in forecasting that appeared in the fall issue of *Weather Times*. My name is Tim Jones, and I recently earned a Master's degree in applied meteorology. I am exploring careers in the renewable energy field, and would like your advice.

   My postgraduate work included quality control...

2. You are contacting someone who works at a professional/trade association:

   Dear Ms. Adams:

   My name is Tim Jones, and I recently earned a Master's degree in applied meteorology. My research into the renewable energy field led me to the Meteorology Association website. As Executive Director, your experience and advice would be very valuable in helping me determine whether renewable energy is the right field for me. I wonder if we can arrange a brief meeting.

   My postgraduate work included quality control...

3. You are contacting someone who works at a professional/trade association *to get referrals to members*:

   Dear Ms. Adams:

   My name is Tim Jones, and I recently earned a Master's degree in applied meteorology. My research into the renewable energy field led me to the Meteorology Association website. I am interested in getting advice about career opportunities. I would like to speak with meteorologists and development directors at companies involved in solar heating, solar thermal power, and hydroelectricity. Please direct me to association members in Massachusetts who might be willing to meet with me.

My postgraduate work included quality control...

4. You are contacting someone who spoke at an industry conference that you did not attend:

Dear Mr. Johnston:

I noticed that you spoke on the topic of renewable energy at the International Meteorology Conference. My name is Tim Jones, and I recently earned a Master's degree in applied meteorology. I am exploring careers in the renewable energy field, and your expertise and advice would be quite valuable to me. Could we arrange a brief meeting?

My postgraduate work included quality control...

5. You are contacting someone you heard speak at an industry conference:

Dear Dr. Lewis:

Last week I heard your very interesting presentation on solar resource mapping at the 10th Annual Meteorology Today conference. My name is Tim Jones, and I recently earned a Master's degree in applied meteorology. I am exploring careers in the renewable energy field, and your expertise and advice would be quite valuable to me. Could we arrange a brief meeting?

My postgraduate work included quality control...

6. You are contacting someone you found via a LinkedIn group:

Dear Ms. Urbano:

My name is Tim Jones, and I am a fellow member of the East Coast Meteorology Professionals group on LinkedIn. Now that I have earned a Master's Degree in applied meteorology, I am exploring careers in the renewable energy field. Could we arrange a brief meeting so that I can get your advice about opportunities in this area?

My postgraduate work included quality control...

How to Make a Follow-up Telephone Call

Keep track of everyone you contact to request informational interviews. Include each person's title, company, telephone number, email, and how you found his or her name. A simple spreadsheet or list will work well. You will need this information to follow up on your inquiries, and possibly later on if you decide to pursue a job in the field.

Following up your inquiry with a telephone call greatly increases your chances of getting a meeting. There is nothing intrusive about this kind of reminder. It demonstrates that you are serious about a meeting, and willing to take action—a trait that is respected by business professionals. If your initial inquiry was sent via email, wait three to four business days before making a follow-up telephone call. If you sent a letter, wait seven to eight business days after the letter was mailed.

Keep your telephone message brief. Remind the person of who you are and why you want to meet. Three or four sentences are sufficient. If you are nervous about calling, write down what you want to say and practice your message until you feel confident.

Practice saying your message out loud, in a conversational tone. You do not want to sound like you are reading a script, even if you are. Leave yourself a voicemail message to hear how you sound to others. Or, make an audio recording.

Be prepared to be surprised by the sound of your own voice at first. This is quite common. You may need to listen to your recording several times just to get used to hearing yourself talk. After that, you can evaluate whether you are speaking too quickly or slowly, with enough inflection in your voice, and in a tone that conveys confidence.

If you call and get the person's voice mail, *leave a message*! They may be on another call or screening incoming messages. If the individual is returning to his desk after a meeting or lunch, he may scan the caller ID list. It looks very unprofessional to make multiple calls without leaving a message.

It is acceptable to suggest one or two times when the person can call back and reach you. The options should be during regular business hours, "You can reach me between 10:00 and 11:30 tomorrow morning, or Wednesday after 3:00pm." It is unprofessional to presume that someone will return your call in the evening or over a weekend. Do *not* say, "I'll be home from the movies tonight at 9:30," or, "I'll be around all weekend." Similarly, avoid complex instructions, such as, "I'll be reachable on Wednesday between 8:30 and 9:15, then from 10:30 to 11:30, again from 12:15 to 1:30, and then probably at 3:00 unless I have to run errands."

If you don't receive a response to a telephone message after three days, you can call again or send an email. If this doesn't work, send one more email or make one more telephone call. If there is still no response, assume that the individual cannot, or is not willing to, meet with you. This is the point to stop making contact. Do not be discouraged if this happens. Some people are simply too busy to accommodate your request. All it means is that you need to move on to the next person. Continuing to call or email would be very annoying and could be considered harassment.

There are four parts to a follow-up telephone message:

1. State your name.

2. Explain why you are calling.

3. Request a meeting.

4. Leave your contact information if you get voicemail.

Some people prefer email to the telephone, so leaving both your telephone number and email address in a voicemail makes it easier for the individual to respond.

Here is a sample telephone follow-up script:

Hello, Mr. Davis, this is Tim Jones. I'm calling to follow up on an email I sent you last week. I'm exploring meteorology careers in renewable energy, and would like your advice. I'm hoping that we can arrange a brief meeting in the next week or two. You can reach me at 617-555-5555 or via email at tjones@isp.com. Thank you. Goodbye.

Notice how this message creates a subtle sense of urgency by suggesting a meeting with two weeks.

Speaking of Voicemail…

Is *your* greeting professional and friendly sounding? Call yourself and listen to your voicemail greeting. Are you mumbling, or speaking so softly or quickly, that callers will have a hard time understanding you? Can you hear people talking, or the sound of a television set, in the background? Is your message very short ("Hi, leave a message") or silly ("How 'ya doing! I'm out hanging with some friends now…")?

When you are looking for a job, the priority is to present yourself in a positive light to potential employers. During your search, use a professional voicemail greeting, "Hello, this is Tim Jones. I can't come to the phone now, so please leave a message and I will return your call as soon as possible."

STEP 4: CONDUCTING THE MEETING

Congratulations! You found contact names, sent query letters, made follow-up calls, and now have scheduled an informational interview. What's left is showing up and asking questions, right?

Not quite. This is *your* meeting, and you must prepare to conduct it in a professional manner. This means dressing in business attire, being prepared with questions to ask, and bringing a pad of paper and pen for taking notes. You should also bring four or five copies of your resume. Materials should be carried in a briefcase, leather tote, or simple portfolio.

Bring the person's telephone number with you, in case you are late. The *only* reason this should happen is because of an unavoidable situation, such as a traffic jam. Poor planning or time management on your part are not acceptable excuses. The Informational Interview Checklist at the end of this chapter includes a section on planning travel.

For an extra edge, you can create a simple business card with your name and contact information. Stationery stores sell inexpensive, die-cut sheets for printing out cards from your home computer. A copy center can design and print cards for you.

Preparing Small Talk and Conversation Starters

Your preparation must also include practicing how to introduce yourself, and being ready with small talk and conversation starters. These are essential for creating a positive first impression and establishing connections with others. In addition to getting career information, your goal is to establish a networking contact if you decide to look for work in the field. If a business professional does not feel comfortable interacting with you, he will not assist you or make referrals.

It is expected that you will engage in *small talk* as you make your way from the reception area to the location of the informational interview. Usually, the interview is in your contact's office or a conference room. Depending on the size of the building, this trip can take a few seconds or several minutes. If you stare at the floor, or the door of the elevator, or respond with one-word answers to questions about the weather or traffic, you will be perceived as odd, unfriendly, or unprepared.

Usually, but not always, you will be escorted from the reception area by someone other than your contact, typically his assistant. This is when you will use your prepared small talk. It consists of comments or observations about neutral topics like the weather or a non-controversial news event, "Beautiful weather we're having," or, "Have you been following the baseball playoffs?" Alternately, you can ask general questions about the individual or the company, "How long have you worked here?" or, "Has WidgetWorks always been in this building?"

If *you* are asked small-talk questions about your ride to the office or your opinion about the weather, answer briefly and positively. This is an exchange of pleasantries, not information. The other person is not interested in a long discourse about the terrible traffic, what happened when you got lost, or how the ridiculously high pollen count affects your sinuses.

Conversation starters are for your contact and used to transition from "greeting to meeting." They lend a conversational air to the discussion that puts people at ease. If you sit down and immediately launch into a string of questions, the other person may feel like he is being interrogated!

Learning how to prepare conversation starters and talking points is a critical skill that you need for informational interviews, job networking, job interviews, and interacting with co-workers after you are hired. The secret is to establish a connection by finding commonalities between you and the other person, or talking points related to the context of your discussion.

Jill arranged an informational interview with the executive director of a large non-profit. "I know all of the questions that I want to ask," she said.

"Great," I replied. "What do you know about her that you can use to establish a connection?"

"Nothing," Jill said, looking confused, "I haven't met her yet."

We took a look at the organization's website, and found a section that contained biographies of the senior staff members, including the executive director. "She went to the same university as I did," Jill said, "and we both grew up in New York City." Voila! In just a few seconds, Jill found two things that she had in common with executive director.

Conversation starters are pieces of information that you can ask the other person about or comment on. These include the individual's participation at an industry event, an award, an unusual career path, volunteer activities, or hobbies. LinkedIn is an excellent source of this type of information.

Here are some examples of conversation starters:

- "I went to Brown University, too."

- "Congratulations on winning the Rodgers Foundation Award!"

- "What did you think of the International Technology Conference?"

- "You started your career in geology; what made you switch to business administration?"

- "How long have you volunteered with The Heart Association?"

- "I enjoyed your article in *Tech Talk*."

- "Was the Documentation Certification program valuable to your career?"

- "I've been thinking about joining the Direct Marketers Association. Would you recommend it?"

Like small talk, conversation starters result in a back-and-forth exchange that typically lasts for two to three turns. You might say, "I noticed that you went to Acme University, too." Your contact responds, "Yes, I majored in communications; how about you?" You say, "My original major was biology. I switched to communications when I decided to pursue a career in marketing. It is a great school." To this your contact responds, "I agree, and serve on the alumni committee. Here's my office, come in and have a seat."

Notice that the questions and responses were about the same topic. Asking a series of unrelated questions could give the impression that you are "grilling" the contact for information, or that you are nervous or disorganized.

Even though the exchange is conversational and friendly, this is still a business meeting. Therefore, it is not appropriate use flattery, to remark about someone's personal appearance, or to mention politics or religion. If you are inquiring about an industry event, choose one that happened within the past 18 months.

Here are examples of what *not* to say:

- "You must be really smart to graduate from Harvard!"

- "You look a lot younger in person."

- "I'm voting democratic in this election; are you?"

- "I saw that you spoke at the Widget conference in 1997."

If you are not able to find commonalities or talking points (some individuals strictly limit information that they share online), or if you are escorted from a reception area by someone other than your contact, you can engage in general small talk.

What to Do When You Arrive

Plan to arrive in the reception area 15 minutes before your scheduled appointment. If you are very early, wait in your car, get a cup of coffee, or otherwise pass the time before making your way into the building. Showing up 45 minutes early for a meeting communicates that you are disorganized or too anxious, and puts a subtle pressure on your contact since they know you are waiting.

Unless it is a very small office, you will first announce yourself to the receptionist. Walk up to the desk, and wait for the individual to look at you. Do not begin speaking if he or she is on the telephone. Smile, introduce yourself, and state who you are meeting with, "Hello, I'm Laura Smith. I have an 11:00 appointment with Michael Miller." It is not customary to shake hands with a receptionist. He or she will let the contact know that you have arrived, and direct you to a seat in the waiting area.

The person who comes out to meet you might be your contact, or that person's assistant or associate. Listen as they introduce themselves to find out.

Regardless of who meets you, it is expected that you will stand up and extend a greeting. The correct way to do this is look at the individual, making eye contact, and smile as you extend your right hand. When you shake hands, the area between your thumb and forefinger should be nestled against the same area on the other person's right hand. Squeeze their hand firmly and say your greeting, "Hello, Michael, I'm Laura Smith. It's nice to meet you."

A weak handshake communicates low confidence. Too much pressure can be painful. Practice a firm, confident handshake.

Smiling is a critical part of this exchange. It conveys friendliness and enthusiasm, and puts people at ease. I consider it a basic job readiness skill. If you are not used to smiling, practice until it becomes automatic, particularly when you are saying hello and goodbye to people.

Begin by smiling in front of a mirror so that you can find the point where you look friendly and relaxed. Pay attention to how your mouth feels and looks. If possible, ask family members to remind you to smile when you see them. Placing a mirror near the telephone is a way to monitor your expression. Smiling changes the sound of your voice. Sales people are taught to smile when they pick up the telephone because they sound friendlier and more enthusiastic.

After you say your greeting, you will be escorted to the meeting location. This is when you should expect to exchange small talk. Sometimes the person escorting you comes to the rescue, recognizing that you may be nervous, and makes the small talk first!

Finally, you are seated in front of your contact, ready to begin the informational interview. It is polite to thank the individual for agreeing to meet with you. Express your enthusiasm. You can say, "Thank you for taking the time to meet with me. I'm eager to get your advice about working in the accounting profession." Then, proceed with your first question.

It is acceptable to take notes during an informational interview. However, do not take so many that you spend more time looking at your pad than at the individual. Do not ask if you can make an audio recording of the meeting.

Be respectful of the individual's time. Informational interviews usually last about 30 minutes. This allows time for roughly six to eight questions. If the discussion is going well and you are uncertain about how much time has passed, ask whether the person has time for one or two more questions. If you plan to ask for referrals (other people to talk to), do so at the end of the interview.

At the conclusion of the meeting, thank the individual again for their time, and ask for a business card, "This has been very helpful, and I appreciate the great advice and referrals. I'll let you know what happens. May I have your card?" Smile, shake hands, say goodbye, and leave.

STEP 5: FOLLOWING UP AFTER THE INFORMATIONAL INTERVIEW
Once you return home, update your contact list or spreadsheet with notes about what happened at the meeting. Remember, you may be renewing contact with this individual in the future.

Always send a written thank you within 48 hours of your meeting. Refer to some of the specific things that you discussed, "Thank you for giving me the website of the regional association chapter. I'll plan on attending their next meeting," "I will contact John Jones, Sarah Smith and Beth Lewis this week and let you know what happens," "I will look into the certification program that you mentioned."

Another way to make a very positive impression, and establish the individual as a networking contact, is to send an update after you have had the chance to follow through on their recommendations.

This is an example of a thank you letter or email following an informational interview:

Dear John:

Thank you very much for all of the advice and suggestions you shared with me at our meeting yesterday. I now have a better understanding of career options in the meteorology field.

The American Meteorology Association sounds like an excellent resource, and I will check out their website this week. As you suggested, I will also get in touch with the Executive Director, Allan Johnson.

I will also contact Dr. Smith at MATs University and Theresa Miller at Solar Products International. It will be interesting to learn about opportunities in research, and also in product development which I hadn't considered previously.

Thank you again, John, for your assistance.

Sincerely,

Timothy Jones

This is an example of an update that would be sent several weeks later:

Dear John:

I'm writing to let you know that I had very productive meetings with Allan Johnson and Dr. Smith. Allan invited me to attend the next association meeting as his guest, and also gave me the names of three association members to contact. Dr. Smith explained some of the current research she is leading, and offered to give me names of people to meet, if I decide to pursue research as a career.

Theresa Miller has been traveling, and we are going to meet next month.

I will keep you updated on my progress!

Sincerely,

Timothy Jones

If the research, querying, preparation, and follow up seem like a lot of work, you're right. However, it is worth the effort. The information and advice will help you decide whether a profession is right for you. The practice you get finding contacts and conducting meetings will increase your confidence during networking activities and on job interviews.

Job Shadowing and Strategic Volunteering

These are two more ways to learn about an occupation.

Job shadowing is when you observe someone at his place of business. Alec, for instance, arranged to shadow a speech language pathologist who worked at a public school, and one who worked in private practice. He spent two hours at each site, watching the practitioners at work. Even though he had done extensive reading about the profession, seeing the professionals in action was very instructive. Alec realized that his interest was not clinical practice, but research.

You can shadow someone for an hour or two, an entire day, and even over several days. This activity is useful when you are exploring jobs that are physical in nature, such as printing press operator, commercial photographer, teacher, or news reporter. Not every occupation lends itself to job shadowing. There is little you could learn watching an accountant or a copywriter that you couldn't discover asking questions at an informational interview. The confidentiality rules that govern some professions, such as psychotherapy, would make job shadowing impossible.

The individual being shadowed is investing a significant amount of time with you. For this reason, you should reach out to people you already know, either to observe them, or to ask for a referral.

Strategic volunteering is when you work without pay for the purpose of experiencing a particular job or industry. It is strategic when you match the volunteer activity to your area of interest. If you were thinking about becoming a veterinary technician, volunteering for a few hours per week at a vet's office would show you what the work is like. Sarah wanted to test her skills at reporting, and volunteered to write bi-weekly articles for her local newspaper.

✓

JOB RESEARCH TEMPLATE

Copy this form for each occupation that you are researching.

Begin by gathering basic information about the job or career that you are interested in from an occupational database such as the Occupational Outlook Handbook (www.bls.gov/ooh).

Name of job/career: _____

Read the description of the nature of the work. What are the primary job tasks? Are there specialties (lawyers, for example, may specialize in civil or criminal law, bankruptcy, or property law, etc.)? What kind of equipment or technology is used?

1. What are the most important hard skills needed for this work?

   _____

   _____

   _____

2. What are the most important soft skills?

   _____

   _____

   _____

3. How is the work environment described? What is the pace like? How many hours per week are typical? How much structure is there?

   _____

   _____

   _____

4. How well do you think you could work in this environment?

_____

_____

_____

5. What kind of education or training do you need? Are you able to acquire any that you lack?

_____

_____

_____

6. How do you see yourself advancing in the field?

_____

_____

_____

7. What types of companies hire people in this field? Which type of companies and/or industries do you prefer?

_____

_____

_____

8. What is the job outlook? Have there been any major changes in the field? How competitive is it? Are certain jobs more abundant than others? If you are new to this work, what are the entry-level jobs?

_____

_____

_____

9. How much can you make? Are the average salaries what you expected? (Note that salaries may be averages, and not necessarily what is paid at the entry-level.)

_____

_____

_____

10. What are the related occupations? Which, if any, do you want to learn more about?

_____

_____

_____

11. What aspects of this occupation are attractive to you?

_____

_____

_____

12. What aspects are you concerned about? Are there any tasks that would be difficult or impossible for you to manage?

_____

_____

_____

13. Based on what you know now, rate your interest in this occupation:

A   I am very interested in this occupation and want to learn more.

B   Looks interesting; I have some concerns but will continue researching.

C   Might be a possibility, but I do not want to actively research it at this time.

D   Take it off the list!

14. If you rated this occupation an A or B, which resources do you want to consult next?

☐ Visit job board(s) and review three to five job posts.

☐ Research occupations on another website, such as O*NET (www.onetonline.org).

☐ Google search the job/career (e.g. "What do veterinarians do?" or "Jobs in the legal field").

☐ Visit the website of a professional association.

☐ Read a professional journal/newsletter/blog.

15. Notes:

_____

_____

_____

_____

_____

✓

INFORMATIONAL INTERVIEW CHECKLIST

Check each item when completed.

- ☐ Reviewed the background of the person I am meeting.

- ☐ Prepared two commonalities or talking points.

- ☐ Briefcase, portfolio, or folder contains: five copies of my resume, a pen and notepad, my list of questions, and the individual's telephone number.

- ☐ I have at least five business cards in my wallet or purse (optional).

- ☐ I am dressed as if this is a job interview: professional attire with matching accessories, shoes shined, and hair neatly styled.

Transportation plan

a) My appointment is on [date]_____
   at [time]_____ am/pm.

b) In order to arrive at the reception desk 15 minutes before my appointment, I need to leave my home at [time]_____ am/pm.

   (Note: if you are traveling during rush hour, or not familiar with the area, schedule extra time.)

c) If I am using an automobile, I will park:

   - ☐ in the company's parking lot.

   - ☐ at a parking garage (location: _____
     _____ cost: _____).

   - ☐ I have enough gasoline for the trip.

   - ☐ I have money for a parking garage.

   - ☐ I have money for tolls.

☐ I have printed driving directions.

☐ I am using a GPS system.

d) ☐ I have cash to cover incidental expenses.

e) ☐ If I am using public transportation, I have the bus/train/subway schedule.

CHAPTER 4

PERSONAL PRESENTATION

In just over a week, Zachary would have his first post-graduation job interview. He sat slumped in his chair, looking at the floor as we discussed interview preparation. "I don't know if you are aware that right now, the message you are sending is that you are not interested in what I have to say," I commented.

Zach took the cue and straightened up. "It's just that all of this stuff is so boring and stupid," he sighed. "I don't know why I should have to pretend to be different than I am."

The "stuff" Zach was referring to concerned nonverbal communication and making the right impression. We were discussing handshakes, small talk, eye contact, what to wear, and how to answer interview questions. My impression was that Zach was overwhelmed, not bored.

The week before, my client Terry and I were role-playing an interview. Terry came into my office, sat down and looked at me without smiling. Pretending to be an interviewer, I started asking her questions. Terry spoke very quickly, and began shifting her head away from me. After a few minutes, her responses were being delivered to the wall.

The *content* of Terry's answers demonstrated her skill as a software programmer. Her rapid, mechanical-sounding speech, lack of eye contact and blank facial expression communicated detachment and lack of interest.

"But I *am* interested," she exclaimed.

"I know," I said, "but your body language is saying the opposite. Interviewers react to what your body language communicates as much as to your words."

In his book *Silent Messages*, Dr. Albert Mehrabian presented his findings about nonverbal communication and emotions. He found that 7 percent of what people communicate about their feelings and attitudes comes from their words; 38 percent comes from the way they say those words; and 55 percent comes from their facial expression (Mehrabian 1981).

Body language is a powerful form of nonverbal communication. In addition to facial expression, it includes your posture, proximity to others, gestures, and the orientation of your body (whether you are turned toward or away from someone).

Communicating Nonverbally, A Practical Guide to Presenting Yourself More Effectively (Young and Travis 2008) identifies other, less obvious forms of nonverbal communication. "Artifacts" are items in our personal space, such as furniture, artwork, and jewelry. "Chronemics" refers to how one's use of time communicates, "how we view others, what our culture values, and how efficient we are" (Young and Travis 2008, p.9). In our culture, habitually arriving late for appointments is interpreted as a lack of respect for the other person's time.

Paralanguage, or the way something is said, includes your volume and tone of voice, rate of speech, and the emphasis you place on a word or phrase (Young and Travis 2008). "You did a *great* job on that" implies work well done. "You did a great job on *that*" is a sarcastic way to indicate that expectations were not met.

If you have difficulty noticing or interpreting nonverbal signals, you know how difficult it is to figure out the expectations, intentions, and motives of other people. *You* are also communicating nonverbally, and this is what gives meaning—intended or not—to your words. Neurotypicals intuitively, and often subconsciously, rely on nonverbal cues to derive meaning from an interaction.

Remember Ed, who had worked for six different law firms within a decade? His outstanding legal knowledge was never in question. The problem was his inability to "fit in." At one firm, he was taken to task for stacking empty soda cans in his office. "It was very embarrassing," Ed said. "It never occurred to me that something like that would hurt my image."

People do not expect to enter a law office and see a stack of empty soda cans. Although it wasn't his intention, Ed's action caused clients to question his judgment and professionalism. His colleagues were concerned that this could damage the firm's reputation.

As a job seeker, it is imperative that you are aware of messages that you are sending nonverbally. At every stage of a job search, you are sending messages that people use to form impressions. Even your choice of resume paper communicates your level of professionalism. The good news is that you can manage how others perceive you.

YOU ARE COMMUNICATING NONVERBALLY THROUGHOUT THE JOB SEARCH

It only takes a few seconds for people to begin forming impressions of each other. They don't have to meet face to face. Imagine that you receive a resume that contains multiple typographical errors. How confident would you feel about the individual's ability to produce accurate work?

Whether a first impression is accurate or not, it can be difficult to change. Clients sometimes challenge me about what they consider to be trivial concerns. If you have outstanding skills, they ask, what difference does it make if your resume contains typos or you forget to smile? Who cares if you appear anxious as long as you get your work done?

In the neurotypical workplace, things like this make a big difference. They can prevent you from getting an interview or a job offer, and keep you from being promoted once you are hired.

What follows are tips about how to present yourself as professional, enthusiastic, confident, and reliable at various stages of the job search.

RESUME AND COVER LETTER

Writing effective resumes and cover letters will be covered in depth in the next chapter. My purpose in mentioning them here is to describe how they relate to your personal presentation.

Your goal when submitting these documents is an interview. Employers receive dozens, and sometimes hundreds, of resumes in response to a posted opening. In order to narrow the candidate pool to a manageable number, resumes that are not professional in appearance are eliminated.

Typographical and grammatical errors make the screener's job easy: these applicants are *out*. Mistakes like these send the message that you are careless, and that your work will contain errors, too. I have had clients show me resumes that state they are detail oriented, yet contain multiple typos!

Proofread your resume carefully. Ideally, you should have one or two other people proofread it as well. Read your cover letter before sending it out so that you can correct any errors.

Don't use unusual, hard-to-read fonts. Rather than make your resume stand out, they suggest someone who is odd or has poor judgment. Employers typically spend *seconds* scanning a resume. If it is hard to read, they will discard it. Hard copies of your resume and cover letter should be printed on high-quality, watermarked resume paper. They should be mailed in matching, type-written envelopes. Stationery stores carry paper specifically for resumes and cover letters. Acceptable colors are white, cream, or tan.

Plain bond photocopy paper is not suitable. It communicates that you do not care enough to invest in making a good impression. Brightly colored paper is unprofessional and will land your resume in the "no" pile.

PERSONAL APPEARANCE

Recently, I was speaking to a group about interviewing skills. During my presentation, I showed them a photo of a sleepy-eyed hippie who had long, stringy hair held back by a headband. Thin wire spectacles with blue-tinted lenses sat at the end of his nose. He was dressed in a tie-dyed tee shirt, and was making the peace sign.

Everyone laughed because this was such an exaggerated example of inappropriate interview attire. Still, it made my point. People react to your physical appearance.

At a job interview, the wrong attire makes the statement, "This person will not fit in." This is true whether you are dressed too casually or too formally. The general rule for interviews is to dress one level above how you would as an employee. Thus, if employees are expected to wear dress pants, a dress shirt, and blazer, at an interview, you would wear dress pants, a dress shirt, blazer, and necktie.

Overdressing implies that you don't fit with a company's culture, or understand the way it does business. What defines overdressed will vary by job or industry. A formal suit and tie would raise questions at a high technology company, but be expected at an investment bank. A woman interviewing for a job as a pre-school teacher would look out of place in a silk blouse, linen skirt, high heels, and sophisticated jewelry.

Women should choose classic, conservative clothing in dark or neutral colors. A suit is not required for interviews. Alternatives are trousers or a skirt with a dress blouse or sweater, or a jacket worn over a blouse or sweater. Keep jewelry and make-up conservative and minimal. Short skirts, heels over three inches, and low necklines are to be avoided.

Men and women should wear closed-toe shoes (not evening shoes) that are clean and shined. Accessories should match. Men wearing brown shoes should wear a brown belt; ladies should carry a medium-size handbag in a color that complements their shoes. Sales associates at department and specialty clothing stores can help you choose a professional outfit.

Basic hygiene bears a mention, since people who are unclean are not pleasant to be around. Your clothing should be clean and pressed. Wrinkles and stains make a terrible impression. Bathe either the night before or the day of your interview. Your hair should be clean and neatly styled.

Your personal presentation extends to the items that you carry with you. A bulging briefcase or multiple tote bags packed with file folders looks disorganized. Take only those items that you need to a meeting or interview. Typically these will be extra copies of your resume, a pad and pen for note taking, business cards, and samples of your work (if applicable). Transport these items in a briefcase or portfolio.

SPEECH

When you speak, people must not only hear the words that you say, but that you are confident and enthusiastic. The *way* that you say things, not the words themselves, has the greatest influence on the message you send. The ability to communicate is one of the top skills employers want in their employees.

People make inferences about your internal state based on your tempo and volume. Talking too quickly is seen as a sign of nervousness; speaking too softly suggests a lack of confidence. If your volume is too loud, people will read this as a lack of awareness of your surroundings, and imagine that if you were hired, you would disturb your co-workers.

Monotone speech—where there is no change in tone or inflection—communicates low energy and indifference. It can negatively impact your ability to get hired. If this is a problem for you, consider utilizing the services of a speech language pathologist.

Words *do* have an influence on how you are perceived. Language that is too formal or pretentious, whether written or spoken, will be interpreted as arrogance, which is a turn off to employers. One young man, when asked about his weaknesses, told an interviewer that he had a tendency to "bloviate." Another announced in a cover letter, "Attached herewith for your perusal is a resume, which enumerates my qualifications for the aforementioned position." Avoid using words that make you seem unfriendly and unapproachable.

Interrupting is universally considered rude. It is also associated with being a poor listener, an undesirable trait in any workplace.

Chewing gum or eating candy during an interview demonstrates poor manners and a lack of professionalism.

FACIAL EXPRESSION

I consider smiling to be a basic job readiness skill. Sitting stone-faced at an interview will almost certainly disqualify you as a candidate. It makes you appear unfriendly and disinterested—two big strikes against any potential employee.

Your goal is a comfortable smile that looks genuine. You do not need to walk around with a large, goofy grin. Practice in front of a mirror to discover what works for you. The two critical times to smile are when you meet someone, and when you say goodbye. During interviews, smiles can punctuate descriptions of your background, and indicate your interest in what the interviewer is saying. There are no specific rules governing exactly when and how much to smile. Making a video recording of your practice interview sessions will give you an idea of how others see you.

Facing another person and making eye contact are fundamental ways to show that you are engaged in a conversation. Some of my clients say that eye contact as painful, completely distracting, or exhausting. Looking at the space between a person's eyebrows is a way to approximate eye contact. Making too much eye contact, or staring, is also a problem. A long, unbroken gaze is unsettling and could be considered aggressive and hostile.

If you have significant difficulty maintaining the right amount of eye contact, consider disclosing the reason during an interview. Disclosure and workplace accommodations will be discussed in Chapter 8.

BODY LANGUAGE

Mitch was surprised to learn at his performance review that he had been sending unintended messages with his body language. He received a low score for collaboration, in part because he did not participate in meetings. Not only did Mitch not share his ideas, but he spent most of the time looking at his notepad. He hadn't realized that by not looking at people when they spoke, he gave the impression that he wasn't listening.

"Using your body to establish a physical presence" is discussed in *Social Thinking at Work, Why Should I Care?* (Winner and Crooke 2011, p.74). During interviews, sit up straight and orient your face and body toward the person with whom you are conversing. Slouching says that you are bored. Nodding your head up and down slightly is a visual cue that you are paying attention to what is being said. Leaning forward slightly in your chair, toward the interviewer, is a subtle way of showing attention and interest.

Your gaze indicates what you are thinking about (Winner and Crooke 2011). Looking at your watch or out of the window, or fiddling with objects, are signals that you are distracted. Would you be excited about working with someone who was more interested in a stapler than you?

A firm, confident handshake is another basic job readiness skill. Greetings were discussed in the section on informational interviewing. Practice this essential piece of business etiquette until it is automatic.

ACTIONS AND BEHAVIORS

Kelly's informational interview was a disaster. She was exploring technical writing and had a meeting with the head of the documentation department of an information technology company.

On the morning of the informational interview, Kelly overslept. Managing to get out of the house only a few minutes late, she realized when she reached the highway that she had not factored rush-hour traffic into her drive-time estimate. She felt grateful to arrive just ten minutes late for the meeting.

Once seated, Kelly became agitated. She realized that she had forgotten to bring her list of informational interview questions. When her contact asked, "What do you know about the products that we support?" Kelly drew a complete blank. She hadn't done any research on the company. At one point, Kelly became so flustered that she forgot why she was there and asked whether there were any job openings!

There were two consequences to Kelly's lack of preparation: she didn't learn much from her informational interview; she also gave a potentially valuable networking contact the impression that she was scattered and disorganized. This was hardly the profile of a serious professional.

Being late, forgetting items and not being prepared will be interpreted as laziness, lack of motivation or disorganization. Being prepared shows that you take your job search seriously, and that you respect the time others invest in you.

CHAPTER 5

MARKETING YOURSELF TO EMPLOYERS

UNDERSTANDING THE EMPLOYER'S PERSPECTIVE

Getting a job means marketing yourself to employers.

This idea brings up anxiety and resistance in nearly all of my clients. They worry that marketing means exaggerating their skills, bragging about their accomplishments, pretending to be someone they're not, or flat out lying.

My perspective is different. Before I started coaching, I worked for many years at companies where I managed a staff and made hiring decisions. Filling an open position was always a long, time-consuming process. The hours that were spent screening candidates and conducting interviews were, of course, on top of my regular work. After someone was hired, there would be many more hours devoted to training. Whenever I had an opening, my objective was to find the best person in the shortest time possible.

First, I had to locate individuals with the right skills and experience. At my last job, I worked in a small, specialized field. Although I would have preferred applicants with experience in the industry, that requirement would significantly reduce the qualified candidate pool. For me, specific industry experience was a preferred, not a required, attribute. However, I did have other criteria that were essential.

My co-workers were encouraged to refer people they knew who were interested. This strategy had a good chance of attracting the best person. My co-workers knew the company, how we did business, and my management style. They would only approach people they believed were a match. I also let business colleagues outside of the company know about my opening. My colleagues had good judgment. I always considered people they recommended.

The job opening would also be advertised on the major internet job boards, in local newspapers, and on websites of relevant professional associations. I notified local job-seeker networking groups. At that time, there was no internet business networking site like LinkedIn. Otherwise, I would have posted the opening to relevant special interest groups on the internet. My company did not have the budget to pay an outside recruiter to find prospective candidates.

It didn't take long to start receiving resumes from the internet job boards. Lots and lots of resumes. Even though they were screened by the human resources department, I would still be handed large stacks to review. I didn't have time to read all of them, so I skimmed the resumes and cover letters, pulling out the candidates who met my criteria. It amazed me to receive so many responses from people who clearly were not qualified. "Didn't they read the job post?" I wondered. Some resumes were so confusing I couldn't tell if the candidate had the right experience. These went into the "no" pile. So did the multi-page documents—too many details to wade through. Resumes with typos or inconsistent formatting, as well as gimmicky approaches involving songs and poems, were also removed from consideration.

Next, I would go through the resumes in my "yes" pile, and read them carefully. There were still far too many people to interview. This time, I was more critical in my evaluation. I discarded some and put others in a "maybe" pile. The candidates that got my attention—and were invited for interviews—made it easy for me to see the match between my requirements and their abilities. They also showed an interest in the company and its products and services. When I was through, my list of top candidates typically numbered ten or fewer.

My next task was to narrow this pool even further by screening the applicants on the telephone. This enabled me to get a better understanding of their experience, personality, and the type of job they wanted. I asked about each candidate's salary range to make sure that it was in line with what we could pay. Each person was given a brief description of the company and the job. I would invite between three to five people for face-to-face interviews.

Once, when I needed to hire a marketing manager, a person on my staff recommended one of her former colleagues. The two women had not worked together for almost a decade, but stayed in touch periodically. The colleague had recently been laid off, and let her acquaintances know that she was looking for a new job. Since my staff member was very good at her job, her recommendation carried a lot of weight. I contacted her former colleague that day to arrange an interview.

The colleague had all of the required experience, and asked good questions about the job and our company. She was enthusiastic and struck me as someone who would work well with other people. I offered her the job on the spot.

The marketing manager job was never advertised.

I share this experience to help you better understand an employer's perspective on hiring. Although different companies will have their own procedures for filling openings, the basic process is the same. Hiring managers prefer to find qualified candidates through referrals because it saves a lot of time. They will scan your resume quickly. If they do not see that you meet their criteria, your resume will be set aside.

There are three parts to marketing yourself to employers. The first is creating targeted materials that clearly describe the benefits that you offer an employer—in other words, cover letters and resumes. The second is creating a plan for getting your resume into the hands of a hiring manager who needs what you have to offer. The third is demonstrating that you are the right person for the job during a face-to-face interview.

This chapter focuses on creating the basic marketing tools: resumes and cover letters. The next chapter discusses how to develop a job search plan. Chapter 7 explains how to communicate your abilities during interviews.

IS IT LYING OR MARKETING?

You do not have to be highly animated, loud or extroverted to effectively market yourself. Nor do you have to lie. Marketing is about prioritizing and editing information about your background so that you highlight capabilities that are relevant to the job you are seeking now.

Initially, Tim did not understand this concept. "I don't want to lie," he said. We were brainstorming answers to common interview questions. One that always gave Tim trouble was, "What are your weaknesses?" At various times, Tim had replied, "My self-confidence is low," "I don't like working in groups," "I can't make small talk," and, "I'm not a morning person."

Although these replies were honest, they sent the wrong message to an employer. Companies want employees who are confident about their abilities, can get along with others, and will arrive at work on time. It seemed like an impossible paradox to Tim. He didn't want to lie, but if he told the truth, he wouldn't get hired.

We discussed how Tim was being very literal and rigid in the way he defined lying. To him, something was either true or false. Period. However, situations are usually not that black and white. Depending on the context, there can be several honest responses to a question.

It was true that Tim's self-confidence was low. Within the context of a job interview, this is not a good answer. Interviews are where you demonstrate the results you can achieve for an employer. However, within the context of a coaching session, discussing low self-confidence is desirable. The purpose of coaching is learning how to work around limitations and reach goals.

Thinking about situational context allows you to edit what you say and do based on relevancy, rather than what first comes to mind. Now, when Tim is asked about weaknesses at interviews, he truthfully replies that he can be a perfectionist, but has learned that meeting deadlines is more important than fussing over every detail. In this answer, he applies some marketing savvy by explaining how he manages his weakness so that it wouldn't interfere with his job performance.

Here is another way to think about The Truth. If other people misunderstand your message, motive or intention, then what they have learned from you really isn't true. Truth depends on situational context.

There is a difference between bragging and discussing your accomplishments. A braggart talks about himself in a way that is self-aggrandizing. He may exaggerate his abilities and present himself as superior. "I used my outstanding intellect and tremendous writing ability to produce the best brochure the marketing director had ever seen," is an example of bragging.

It is expected that you will describe your capabilities and positive attributes, and give examples of results that you have achieved, on your resume. Otherwise, a hiring manager has no way of knowing whether you can do the job. It is not conceited to say, "I'm skilled at analyzing data about customer buying habits, and was able to predict with 98 percent accuracy the first quarter sales of a new Widget." It is effective self-marketing.

Adopting a marketing perspective will help you to identify jobs for which you qualify. This enabled Keith to focus on the right details when reading job posts. Previously, he applied to many jobs for which he had the technical qualifications, but not the required healthcare industry experience. We will discuss how to decode job posts later in this chapter.

YOUR RESUME IS A MARKETING TOOL

A resume is a marketing document. It must quickly and clearly communicate how your skills and experience fill an employer's need. It is *not* a log of every task that you performed at every job you have ever held. It should only include information that is relevant to the job you are seeking *now*.

The pragmatic nature of people with Asperger's Syndrome can result in resumes that contain too few, too many, or the wrong details. Dan summarized two years of writing experience in one brief sentence on his resume. "Employers know what writers do," he said. I explained, "They don't know that you researched topics, found experts to interview, wrote feature articles, or that you won a writing award, unless you tell them."

Jeff had less than ten years of work experience and a resume that was five pages long. He repeated, word for word, a description of basic web development tasks for each of his four jobs. Rather than highlight his skills, this made his resume very hard to read.

Jeff's resume also included jobs that he had during college, even though they were not related to his current work. If Jeff had been a new graduate, these jobs would have demonstrated that he had practical work experience, which is always valuable when you are starting out. But Jeff was an experienced web development professional. In this situation, the college jobs were not relevant.

A powerful resume does more than state what you did. It describes *the results that you achieved*. Whenever possible, give examples of how you saved a company money or time, improved efficiency, increased sales, or enhanced product performance.

Which description in each of these sets is more impressive?

"Commercial telephone and data wiring."

or

"Troubleshoot complex systems to efficiently install telephone and data wiring."

*

"Wrote articles."

or

"Interviewed information systems managers and wrote 15 feature articles on data center management."

*

"Created direct marketing packages."

or

"Created direct marketing campaigns that increased sales by 16 percent."

*

"Operated cash register."

or

"Accurately handled approximately 35 transactions per hour."

Notice how the second entries describe specific skills, and include results. Initially, Sharon described her experience as a reporter this way:

Wrote for local weekly newspapers owned by The Tri-State Media Network (division of News Times Group, Inc.). Covered a number of towns in the Union, Lake Monroe, and Sunny Valley regions. Wrote for the *Union Daily Mirror* and *Monroe Valley Daily News*. Generated most story ideas assigned. Excelled at feature stories.

Although the information in the description is accurate, the focus is on the wrong details. The emphasis is on the newspapers, when it should be on Sharon's skills and accomplishments. After we discussed important qualifications for a reporter, Sharon wrote a new description:

Developed story ideas for two weekly newspapers. Interviewed area business people and wrote two to three feature articles per week. Edited print stories for online editions. Built strong relationships with community members of diverse ages, backgrounds, and personalities.

Notice how this version highlights Sharon's skills: the ability to think of ideas for stories, conduct interviews, compose feature pieces, meet deadlines, edit her work for the internet, and establish rapport with a variety of different people. This is relevant to an employer.

HOW TO WRITE AN EFFECTIVE RESUME

There is no *one right way* to write a resume. There are hundreds of books and thousands of websites on the subject. Even experts disagree about the optimal length, nuances of formatting, and whether there should be an objective. However, there are guidelines on presenting yourself as skilled and professional.

The two basic resume formats are chronological and functional. A chronological resume lists your job experience in reverse chronological order: your most recent job is listed first. A functional resume describes your abilities and accomplishments, followed by a list of specific jobs. There are pros and cons with each format.

On the plus side, a chronological resume makes it easy for an employer to see your career progression. The description of your most recent job is typically the most detailed. Each successive position contains fewer details, since past experience is usually, but not always, less relevant. A drawback to this format is that the sequential order will make it very obvious if you have had multiple jobs or frequent short-term employment. Your major accomplishments may not have been at your most recent position, and will not be prominently featured.

A functional resumes draws attention to your talents, skills, and achievements. Rather than associating them with specific jobs, they are grouped as a summary of abilities. Specific jobs are briefly noted in the next section of the resume. The entries typically include the job title, company, and dates of employment. The primary benefit of this format is that it can disguise a checkered work history. However, it also makes it hard for an employer to see your career progression. Choosing a functional format may flag you as someone who has held multiple or short-term jobs.

Many job seekers combine the two formats, summarizing their important skills and achievements first, and then describing specific jobs in reverse chronological order.

DEMONSTRATE YOUR QUALIFICATIONS

An effective resume demonstrates that you have the experience and skills needed to do a specific job.

To identify key requirements, review your preliminary career research and notes from informational interviews. (If you skipped the career research step, I strongly suggest that you do this work now. The information will enable you to write a stronger resume, *and* increase your self-confidence and performance during job interviews.) You can also visit internet job boards and read several posts to see what requirements employers emphasize. Refer back to your lists (from Chapter 2) of your top talents and skills.

Once you know the primary job requirements, find examples from your own experience that prove your knowledge and capabilities. Ask yourself, "How do I know that I can do…" or, "What makes me good at doing…" The examples can be from a current or previous job, volunteer work, an internship, college projects, or activities, such as participating on a committee.

Evidence of your ability can also come from an achievement or third-party endorsement, such as: winning an award, having an article published, speaking at an event, receiving a compliment from a supervisor, or getting promoted.

You do not need to demonstrate qualifications for *every* single aspect of a job, just the primary ones. If you have difficulty figuring out what those are, get help from a family member, friend, or professional.

Here is an example of how to demonstrate abilities using information in a job post for a presentation specialist.

1. Underline the critical skills:

   The Presentation Specialist will produce high-level presentations and proposals that convey benefits of our online marketing services in an aesthetically pleasing and persuasive way. This position is meant for a driven, detail-oriented individual who can express quantitative data as engaging visualizations. Due to the strict deadlines we maintain for our clients, the individual must not only work under pressure, but also effectively multitask to account for priorities that can shift hourly.❷ We require that this individual be an expert in PowerPoint❸ and have working knowledge of the suite of Microsoft and Adobe programs.

2. Demonstrate that you have the required skills:

   ❶ Have five years of graphic design experience; create presentations that highlight sales and market data for the senior management team; incorporate photography and other visual elements.

   ❷ Handle an average of four "emergency" requests per week from the marketing group without missing deadlines.

   ❸ Create PowerPoint presentations that incorporate customized animation with multiple motion paths, customized sound, and embedded video.

3. How the skills would look on your resume:

   Graphics professional with five years' experience designing marketing collateral including advertisements, direct mail, websites, email and social media campaigns, sales presentations, websites and landing pages. Develop and execute an average of 30 projects per month; adhere to strict deadlines and budgets. Utilize Adobe Illustrator, Photoshop, InDesign; Microsoft PowerPoint MVP; certified in CSS and HTML.

Review samples of resumes that are specific to your field to get ideas about how to present your qualifications. Read through several examples and note what information is standard. Copywriters and graphic design professionals, for instance, often include links to samples of their work. Individuals pursuing academia are expected to submit a curriculum vitae (CV). You can find sample resumes in books and on the internet by searching, "sample resumes for [job title]."

THE BASIC RESUME FORMAT

This is the basic format of a chronological resume. It can be adapted to fit your situation and preferences. If you are pursuing two different types of jobs, you will need to create separate versions of your resume that are specifically targeted.

1. Your contact information, including address, telephone number, and email. Use a professional email address—employers will not be interested in contacting loafer@isp.com.

2. An objective or summary of qualifications. This should make it immediately clear what type of job you are seeking.

   An *objective* states, in one or two sentences, the job you want and the benefits you bring to an employer. Avoid self-serving objectives. Employers are not interested in helping you hone your craft, increase your experience, or learn a new industry. Here is the resume objective of Taylor, a client with Nonverbal Learning Disorder, who wants to do fundraising for a non-profit:

   Objective: Development position where strong relationship-building, public speaking, and writing skills will be utilized to increase charitable contributions from individuals, businesses, and foundations.

   A *summary* of qualifications is a synopsis of experience and abilities. It is typically three to five sentences in length. Adam's summary reads:

   Experienced researcher and writer of historical biographies. Skilled at utilizing census data, biographical dictionaries, deeds, wills, and other archival material to produce richly detailed narratives. Efficiently produce feature articles, commemorative booklets, websites, and book-length manuscripts.

3. The next section describes your work experience. Paid jobs, internships, and volunteer experience can be included. Recent graduates can

highlight school projects and activities, particularly those that demonstrate teamwork, problem solving, and creativity.

Each job has its own, separate entry. It begins with your job title and the name of the company where you work/have worked. My preference is to place length of employment at the end of an entry. It can be stated from month/year to month/year (May, 2007–October, 2009) or year to year (2008–2010). Whichever format you choose, use it consistently throughout your resume.

The body of the entry describes primary job responsibilities, skills used, and results achieved.

Use key words that match those commonly used in job posts. Think about how you provided a benefit to the employer. Did you save or make money for the organization, save time, increase efficiency, exceed quota, produce very accurate work? Say so!

Entries should be brief and contain information that is relevant to your current employment goal. It is not necessary to state the obvious. It is understood that a receptionist answers the telephone. Receptionists who know how to market their skills are those who, "provide first-line security by checking visitor IDs."

4. Other relevant information includes awards, association memberships, authorship of a blog or article, and speaking engagements. Choose pertinent activities and accomplishments. If you are a writer, mentioning that you produce a blog related to a hobby is relevant. If you are an engineer, it is not.

Stick to the recent past. Achievements from high school are not appropriate if you have several years of work experience. Exceptions would be achievements that demonstrate outstanding intellect, leadership, or perseverance, such as earning the designation of Eagle Scout.

Skip information that is controversial or polarizing. Links to your reviews of heavy metal music, or statements of your political or religious affiliations are not appropriate unless they specifically relate to your occupation.

5. Education is typically mentioned last on a resume. The name of the school and your major are usually sufficient. Include a GPA if it is 3.5 or better. If you are a new graduate with little or no work experience, your academic achievements will be emphasized in the body of your

resume. If you have completed training for a new career, but do not have experience in the field, leading with your educational credentials could be a wise marketing strategy.

BIG RESUME MISTAKES TO AVOID

Organizations can receive hundreds of resumes in response to posted openings. Even if software is used for screening applicants, at some point your resume will pass before human eyes. These are common mistakes that could land your resume in the "no" pile.

Vague Objective or Summary of Qualifications

The person reading your resume should understand what you do… immediately. Avoid a vague objective such as, "To obtain employment with a reputable business where I can apply my education and experience to an employer's benefit." This says nothing about your skills or the type of position you are looking for. Neither does, "To obtain an entry-level position in a sports club." *What* position? If your objective is, "any job in marketing," you are suggesting that you do not know for what you are qualified. The employer will not spend time figuring that out.

Too Much Information

The purpose of this document is to highlight skills and accomplishments that are relevant to the job you want *now*. I have seen resumes that are four and five pages long, packed with details from jobs going back 15 or 20 years. This amount of detail makes it difficult to understand your capabilities and could raise questions about your ability to prioritize.

In most cases, one page is the ideal length. Individuals in more senior roles may have two-page resumes. Your most recent experience is considered the most relevant, which is why jobs held 15 years ago or more should not be included. If you believe your early experience to be critical, several positions can be consolidated under one subheading. Jill, for example, listed three technical writing jobs under the category of "Early Writing Experience," summarizing them all in two sentences.

Not Enough Information

Peter summed up his three years at a historical association with one word: researcher. This did not provide enough information about his abilities. He revised his description to read, "Conducted primary research using journal databases, monographs, library materials, and the internet."

Empty Phrases and Qualifiers

Anything that does not communicate your value to an employer does not belong on your resume. "Was trained in, and performed, the administrator job," is an empty phrase that states the obvious: employees are assumed to be trained to carry out job duties. Qualifiers modify your proficiency in a certain area, for instance, "limited experience with," "some knowledge of," "minimal use of." If you feel the need to qualify a skill, it probably shouldn't be on your resume.

Affected Language

Very formal language and esoteric words make you seem pompous and unapproachable. Can you imagine trying to have a conversation with an individual who is, "Seeking heretofore an opportunity so oriented as to incorporate numeric acumen that will ultimately lead to application of more rarefied facets of financial management"?!

The Disconnect

After several unsuccessful engineering jobs and an eight-year stint working at a local convenience store, Jack retrained as a paralegal. His resume began with a clear objective, a description of his training program, and highlights from his coursework. Next, under the heading "Work Experience," the first entry was "Night Watchman."

Screech! That is the sound of incongruity stopping a reader in his tracks. Jack's part-time job as a night watchman was not at all related to the paralegal profession. In this case, a chronological resume format didn't work. Jack and I reworked his resume so that "Paralegal Experience" was the first heading after his objective and schooling. The entries included six months of part-time experience at a local law firm, and volunteer work at a non-profit law center.

Errors

It is strongly recommended that you have at least two other people proofread your resume. Typographical or grammatical errors will probably disqualify you as a candidate. Review the rules of capitalization. However, grammar rules do not apply to the abbreviated sentence structure commonly used in resumes.

Formatting Inconsistencies

These, and odd, hard-to-read fonts look sloppy, and give the impression of carelessness or cluelessness. Choose a simple, easy-to-read font, such as Times New Roman, in 11pt or 12pt. Bold-face fonts for subheadings (such as "Work Experience"), and your title and company name, make the document easier to read. Margins at the top, bottom and sides should be at least three-quarters of an inch. Very small margins look unprofessional, and may result in words being cut off when the recipient prints the document.

Avoid complex tabs and multiple columns. Scanning software may not pick up these settings, and render the document unreadable to the scanner, a person, or both. It bears repeating that your email address should be professional, for example, your first initial and last name. If necessary, create a separate email for correspondence related to your job search. Some email addresses, like gmail or hotmail are considered to be less professional.

If you send your resume electronically, choose a professional file name. "Third version of resume," or, "Bookkeeping Resume," tip an employer off that you are looking in several different areas. "Resume of Tim Jones," or, "T Jones Bookkeeper," are better choices.

DECODING THE LANGUAGE OF JOB OPENINGS

Adam couldn't find appropriate job openings, even though he had skills that were in demand. I discovered that he disqualified himself from positions that called for "good people skills"—pretty much every job! "I have Asperger's Syndrome," he said, "I *know* that my people skills aren't very good."

Laura developed a mathematical formula to determine whether she was qualified to be a technical documentation writer. The formula was based on statistics about the average number of resumes that must be sent to get an interview, and the average number of interviews it takes to get a job offer. Laura concluded that if she sent a certain number of resumes and did not get an interview, it would mean that she was not qualified.

Both Adam and Laura were using the wrong details to decide whether they qualified for particular jobs or not. In Adam's case, he missed opportunities because he didn't realize that "good people skills" is a relative term that can mean different qualities depending on a job, and industry, and even within a company. Laura applied to many positions that she was not qualified for because she wasn't looking at whether her skills and experience matched an employer's requirements.

Learning to interpret the language of job posts will assist you during several stages of a job search. It saves time and effort when you apply only to jobs for which you are qualified. Understanding key skills helps you write targeted resumes and cover letters, and prepare responses to interview questions that emphasize how you fill an employer's need.

During preliminary career research, the information in job openings will help you determine whether a profession is a good match for your interests and abilities.

A job opening typically represents an employer's ideal. Most do not expect to find candidates who meet every single one of the listed criteria. Thus, the description is a mix of required and nice-to-have skills and experience.

In addition to describing primary job tasks and needed skills, there is information about necessary skill levels, amount and type of experience, and characteristics of the work environment.

The most important criteria are listed first. Non-negotiable requirements are identified by phrases like:

- "extensive/verifiable experience in…"

- "must include…"

- "do not apply unless you meet these requirements."

Negotiable items are described with phrases such as:

- "preferred…"

- "desired…"

- "the ideal candidate will have…"

- "…is a plus"

- "should be familiar with…"

Primary job tasks are described first, followed by a list of the specific skills that the employer believes are needed to carry out the job duties. Tasks and skills that are considered to be obvious or implied will not be spelled out. For example, it is assumed that a job seeker will know that "reception and administrative duties for a busy car dealership" includes the ability to greet customers with a smile and pleasant greeting, operate a multi-line telephone system and basic office equipment, such as a photocopier, and organize files and paperwork.

The level of proficiency is also described. Phrases such as the following indicate that a basic understanding is needed:

- "working knowledge of…"

- "some experience with…"

- "familiarity with…"

Phrases like the following indicate the advanced ability required:

- "extensive experience in…"

- "expert ability to…"

- "strong knowledge of…"

- "in-depth experience in…."

- "proven track record in…"

Some positions require that a candidate have experience in a particular industry in order to qualify. This is true for many jobs in healthcare and information technology. If industry-specific experience is described with non-negotiable terms, it means that the employer is not willing to provide training.

Most openings specify the number of years of experience that are either desired or required. The range is not absolute. You should match your experience to the seniority level of the job. Someone with 19 months of experience should apply for a job requesting two years, since a few months do not make a difference in one's level of experience. However, a position that requires ten or more years of experience is mid- to senior-level, for which an applicant with three years of experience is not qualified.

Job titles also provide clues about scope of responsibilities and level of experience. However, there can be a significant variance in meaning depending on an occupation, industry, and the size of the company. In very small firms, where a department may comprise a single person, the responsibilities of a director will be quite different from those of someone with the same title in a company with thousands of employees.

Part of your job and career research should include understanding the norms with your occupation of interest. Generally, an associate is a junior-level position responsible for executing tasks. Managers oversee the work of others, who may or may not report to the manager, and are responsible for smooth departmental operation. Directors are responsible for the work of multiple managers and functions within an organization. Vice presidents are part of the management team, and accountable for an organization's financial performance and strategic initiatives.

Job openings also provide clues about the work environment itself. Since the right environment can be so important for a person with Asperger's Syndrome, you will want to pay particular attention to these references.

Phrases that indicate a pressured environment include:

- "deadline-driven environment"

- "a complex organization"

- "hectic"

- "fast paced"

- "high-pressure."

A job that requires you to "maintain a sense of humor" involves stress, frustration, and demanding co-workers.

Jobs that require the following traits are for people who can manage priorities and projects with minimal guidance and supervision:

- "a self-starter"

- "take charge individual"

- "the ability to work independently"

- "the ability to train quickly."

Do not assume that you are not qualified for jobs requiring good people skills, teamwork, and the ability to multitask. These can mean very different things depending on a job, industry, or company, you should not assume that you are not qualified. After all, a librarian at the Boston Public Library will do much more multitasking and interact with many more individuals than one at the library in Stow, Massachusetts (population 6,000).

Additionally, "multitask" can mean rapidly shifting attention between tasks in a short period of time, or being responsible for completing multiple tasks that can be handled one by one. Ian realized that he could not be an interpreter, because it involves simultaneously processing two different languages. Sharon was able to manage being a reporter because she could arrange her days so that interviews and research were done in the mornings, and afternoons were devoted to writing.

The information you gathered during your preliminary research and on informational interviews will help you to determine what these terms mean for a certain occupation.

Phrases that indicate a need to shift attention rapidly throughout the day and prioritize include:

- "juggle multiple projects"

- "manage multiple priorities"

- "work efficiently in fast-paced environment"

- "strong organizational skills."

To define terms like "good people skills" and "teamwork," you need to understand how sophisticated the level of interpersonal interaction will be. I have had clients who are successful sales people because they represent technical products and speak to prospects who also have a high level of technical acumen. Matt is an attorney who specializes in contract law. "Clients ask me questions that are straightforward and answered by strict regulations," he explains. "I could *never* practice divorce law, though, because it involves too many emotions and different points of view."

Take a look at what abilities are emphasized in these openings for an office administrator and a staff accountant:

As the Office Administrator, you are a skilled communicator who is extroverted, personable, and able to actively help build the company culture. Intelligent and ambitious, you thrive in a performance-driven environment where you easily multitask and function independently.

*

Seeking a highly motivated Staff Accountant with exceptional attention to detail. Responsibilities include preparing journal entries, detailed reports, and account reconciliations. This is an excellent opportunity for a candidate who possesses a "can do" attitude and ability to multitask in a fast paced environment.

The office administrator position emphasized interpersonal communication skills with the phrases "skilled communicator," "extroverted, personable," and, "help build the company culture." In contrast, the accountant job highlights hard skills such as "exceptional attention to detail," "journal entries, detailed reports, and account reconciliations." Although the accountant will need to interact with other people inside of the organization, the nature of the communication will be financial.

The need for sophisticated interpersonal communication is denoted by phrases such as "extensive interaction with diverse populations," "work collaboratively," "strong customer service orientation," and, "outstanding communication skills."

I notice that some clients fall into the "look and guess" trap when reading job posts. That is, they look at a job title, or one or two key words in the description, decide that they are qualified, and respond.

Brian earned a liberal arts degree, and decided to enter the workforce with a customer service position. He had worked part time bagging groceries while he was in school, and in the months since graduation, spent a few hours per week doing data entry at his father's small business. Brian was frustrated that the dozens of resumes he sent had so far only resulted in two telephone screening interviews.

Together, Brian and I reviewed some of the job posts to which he had responded. One was for a customer service representative at a very large, multinational firm. I asked Brian how he determined that he was qualified. "Well," he began, "it is customer service, and I had to use customer service skills at the grocery store. A Bachelor's degree is required, which I have. And it says 'ability to pay attention to detail,' and I am detail oriented."

All of these observations were true, however, Brian missed a number of other important requirements. Among them:

- five or more years of customer service experience in Supply Chain and/ or Commercial Sales support highly desirable but not required

- strong MS Office skills in Excel, PowerPoint, Word

- ERP/SAP knowledge desirable

- ability to maintain confidentiality and resolve conflict effectively and professionally.

Brian had never heard of supply chains or commercial sales support; five or more years of this type of experience was described as "highly desirable." He knew how to set up a basic spreadsheet and simple documents, but agreed that his knowledge was nowhere near "strong." He had never heard of ERP (enterprise resource planning) or the German application software company, SAP. When I asked Brian to give me an example of a work situation where he had to resolve conflict, he could not think of one.

"I'm not really seeing the connection between your background and what is required for this job," I said.

Brian sighed, "You're right. I get overwhelmed sometimes by all the information, and just send in my resume."

This did not mean that Brian wasn't qualified for *any* customer service position. However, job title alone does not determine whether you are qualified. Scanning for a few key words or phrases won't, either. You need to consider all of the information that is presented.

By responding to jobs that he was not qualified for, Brian took time away from pursuing viable possibilities. This prolonged his job search, and increased his frustration and discouragement.

There are several things to do in order to determine whether you meet basic job criteria. Read descriptions of the company and job role and responsibilities carefully. Think about what you already know about the nature of the work from your occupational research. If you do not understand most of the requirements, or do not possess the critical skills, you are not qualified.

Think about requirements within the context of the job, not your personal life. Terry used social media and, at first, assumed that this meant she was qualified to carry out "social media campaigns." An internet search of this term revealed that it refers to planning marketing programs on social media platforms.

If you find yourself consistently confused about your qualifications, seek assistance. You may need to do additional research, or revisit the exercise in demonstrating your qualifications.

Any time that you spend now to clarify what you are qualified to do will make it easier to find the right job. Guessing is inefficient, because you might guess wrong. *When you know, you're ready to go.*

HOW TO WRITE A CONVINCING COVER LETTER

A cover letter accompanies your resume. It is not an abbreviated version of your resume. It is personalized correspondence that should convince an employer to read your resume and call you for an interview. To accomplish that, your cover letter must convey your interest in *this* organization and *this* job.

Imagine looking at a group of resumes from candidates who all had the education, skills, and experience you need. Would you want to meet the individuals who sent generic cover letters, or the ones who took the time to learn something about your organization?

Some of my clients complain about the amount of time it takes to personalize cover letters. A well-planned job search involves sending fewer, but better targeted, resumes. Seen from this perspective, customizing cover letters actually saves you time.

A cover letter is no longer than one page. If you are mailing a printed letter, set one-inch margins on all sides.

The basic cover letter format is:

- opening that explains who you are and why you are making contact

- two to four paragraphs summarizing your interest and qualifications

- closing that requests action.

Whenever possible, your cover letter should be addressed to a specific individual. The correct format for this is, "Dear Mr./Ms. [last name]" *followed by a colon*. The next chapter explains how to respond to job openings, and offers ideas about how to identify a hiring manager.

If you are responding to a blind ad, which does not mention an individual or a company, the letter should begin, "To Whom It May Concern" followed by a colon.

Anatomy of a Cover Letter

February 21, 2012

Mr. Paul Heymann, Chief Financial Officer❶
Lesner Enterprises
12 Main Street
Anytown, NY 14761

Dear Mr. Heymann:

I am writing to you on the recommendation of John F. Cena,❷ my accounting professor at the Bentley University Masters of Business Administration program. Professor Cena informed me that Lesner Enterprises is looking to hire financial accounting graduates for your auditor training program.❸ I have enclosed my resume for your consideration.

I graduated with a 3.94 grade point average. In my major, financial accounting, I achieved a 4.0 GPA. Professor Cole thought that my attention to detail, willingness to research Financial Accounting Standards Board General Accounting Principles rulings and overall passion for accounting and auditing would make me an ideal program candidate.❹

Lesner Enterprises is highly regarded as a leader in leather manufacturing. I wear one of your company's jackets in the winter. I recently read in *Forbes Magazine* that your company was number 37 in the Forbes 100 Best Companies list.❺ That is quite an honor.

I will call you next week to see when we can schedule an interview.❻ If it is more convenient, you can reach me at 555-555-5555; email to: philipbrooks@isp.com. ❼

Thank you for your consideration.

Sincerely yours,❽

Philip A. Brooks
365 Maple Street
Mytown, NY 14762

This is an effective letter because:

 It is addressed to a specific individual.

 It mentions a referral from a mutual acquaintance, to establish a connection.

 The reason for writing is stated clearly.

 In three concise sentences, the job seeker highlights the most relevant information about his background: high GPAs, including a perfect 4.0 in financial accounting, and a third-party endorsement of his interest and dedication to the profession.

The job seeker demonstrates interest in this particular company by mentioning a positive personal experience and some research about the organization.

6 Strong closing presumes a positive outcome; follow up is critical. (For a review, see the How to Make a Follow-up Telephone Call in the section on informational interviewing in Chapter 3.)

 The job seeker includes his contact information as a courtesy.

8 Four spaces left for the individual's signature (in blue or black ink).

QUICK TIPS FOR RESUME WRITING

Remember, the purpose of your resume is to quickly and clearly communicate your skills and experience and how they fill an employer's need. The emphasis should be on skills used and results achieved, not a list of tasks. Don't waste space with vague, self-serving objectives or qualifiers like "a little bit of experience." Edit the content with a "marketing mindset," that is, only include information that is relevant to the job you are seeking *now*.

1. Refer to your career research and notes from informational interviews. What are the most important skills and experience needed for this job?

2. Read several job posts and notice what capabilities employers emphasize.

3. Review samples of resumes in your field for ideas about how to present your capabilities. You can find sample resumes in books, and on websites.

4. If you are having difficulty, consult the services of a career professional or coach.

✓

RESUME CHECKLIST

☐ At least two people, including myself, have proofread and eliminated typos and grammatical errors.*

☐ Formatting is consistent throughout, and suitable for computer scanning.

☐ Email address is professional.

☐ Fonts are easy to read (e.g. Times New Roman, 11 or 12pt).

☐ Margins are at least three-quarters of an inch on all sides.

☐ Objective or summary of experience clearly indicates the type of job that I am seeking.

☐ Skills used and results achieved are emphasized.

☐ Content is relevant to the job I am seeking *now*.

☐ Printed copies are on high-quality resume paper and mailed in matching envelopes.

☐ Envelopes are typewritten.

---

* Grammar rules do not apply to the abbreviated sentence structure commonly used in resumes.

✓

COVER LETTER CHECKLIST

- ☐ Salutation is followed by a colon ("Dear Mr. Rodgers:").

- ☐ Letter is addressed to a specific individual whenever possible.

- ☐ Fonts are easy to read (e.g. Times New Roman, 11 or 12pt).

- ☐ Margins are one inch on all sides.

- ☐ Signature is in blue or black ink.

- ☐ Content is customized for each job.

- ☐ Content demonstrates interest and knowledge of the specific company.

- ☐ Closing paragraph requests an interview, states that I will follow up, and includes my contact information.

CHAPTER 6

DEVELOPING AN EFFECTIVE JOB SEARCH PLAN

Finding a job is not simply a matter of sending out resumes. It is a process of finding employers with a need you can fill, and then demonstrating how you fill it.

Joe assumed that because he had a degree in communications, he was qualified for jobs in broadcasting, multimedia, social media, marketing, and editorial. He read job titles, not job descriptions, and applied to many positions for which he lacked basic qualifications.

Remember Laura, who used a mathematical formula to test whether she qualified for technical writing jobs? She based the formula on the average number of resumes that are sent to get an interview, and the average number of interviews it takes to get a job offer. Laura concluded if she sent a certain number of resumes without getting an interview, she was not qualified.

The problem with both of these approaches is that they are based on the wrong details. In Joe's case, he applied to jobs based on too little information. He focused on certain words, without putting them into context. Using social media as a consumer is not the same as creating social media marketing campaigns. Laura interpreted the job search statistics so literally that she missed the big picture. To know whether she was qualified to be a technical documentation writer, she had to match her abilities to the needs of employers.

By this stage, you have identified the job you want, and created a resume that highlights your skills and experience. Now, you need a plan for finding job openings and getting your resume into the hands of hiring managers. This is a marketing campaign.

It makes sense to base your job search plan on an understanding of how people find work. According to *The Career Coward's Guide™ to Job Searching*, approximately one-third of people find jobs through ads, one-third through networking, and one-third by approaching a company directly (Piotrowski

2009, p.5). The career services department of Virginia Tech conducts annual surveys of graduates to learn how they find jobs. Data from 2005 to 2010 shows that, on average, 23 percent find jobs through networking, and 24 percent because they previously worked for the employer (e.g. internship, volunteering, part-time, or summer job, etc.). That is nearly half of the graduates! Less than 10 percent find work through job websites (Career Services at Virginia Tech 2005–2010).

Based on these statistics, it is clear that simply sending your resume in response to posted openings is not very effective. Yet this is the single activity that nearly all my clients use when seeking employment! Adding even one additional strategy will significantly increase your chances of finding a job.

A REVIEW OF JOB SEARCH STRATEGIES

There are many different strategies for finding work. Ideally, your job search plan will include four to six different activities *that you will follow through on consistently*.

There is no point in creating a plan that has actions you won't implement. On the other hand, you must be willing to try new things, which may be uncomfortable at first. The key is to find activities that are effective and manageable.

If walking into a room full of strangers fills you with heart-pounding anxiety, then networking events should not be part of your plan. But, since networking is how most people find jobs, you can try one-on-one networking, or begin by doing some networking online. Three networking strategies for people who are not socially savvy are covered later in this chapter.

Here is a brief review of common job search strategies.

Visit Job Boards and Respond to Posted Openings

People do find jobs this way; however, it takes a lot longer. The big drawback of this method is that you are competing with dozens, if not hundreds, of other applicants. When the candidate pool is large, employers can afford to be very choosy about whom they select for interviews.

Many organizations use computer software to screen incoming resumes. Customizing your resume with key words mentioned in the job post will increase the chances of making it through the first step. Ideally, you will do some research and networking to identify the hiring manager, and contact that person directly. I know of individuals who have set up interviews by letting the hiring manager know that they applied online. Others found the name of the hiring manager through networking contacts. We'll talk about how to find the name of the hiring manager later in this chapter.

Obviously, a personalized approach will not be possible with blind ads that do not include a company name.

Post Your Resume on Job Boards

Recruiters and employers search job boards to find candidates. Many sites allow job seekers to post resumes at no charge. You can do this anonymously if you are currently employed and don't want your employer to find out that you are looking. In addition to large, national job boards, you may be able to post your resume on niche sites that are specialized for specific occupations or industries. The Riley Guide (www.rileyguide.com) is one source for locating niche websites. Professional associations may allow members to post resumes in the career sections of their websites.

If you post your resume, be prepared to receive responses from companies selling services, or recruiting people to fill high-turnover positions, such as insurance sales. Research before you make any commitments, and especially before spending any money. Anyone who contacts you asking for money, or personal information such as your Social Security number, is suspect!

Network Online

The business networking site LinkedIn (www.linkedin.com) is a valuable tool for job seekers. Employers search the database of member profiles to find candidates when they have open positions. Job seekers can also search the database to find individuals for networking. You can create a basic profile at no charge. Using LinkedIn will be discussed in detail later in this chapter.

Register with a Staffing Agency/ies

These firms are retained by companies to find qualified candidates to fill job openings. The agency screens job seekers, and makes referrals based on qualifications. This saves the employer time, hence their willingness to pay the agency a fee.

Agencies often specialize in certain jobs or industries, such as accounting, clerical/administrative support, or healthcare. Some firms place candidates in full-time, staff positions and others place people into part-time or temporary positions. "Temp" assignments can last one day or several months. Often, companies seek temps during busy seasons or to cover for employees on leave of absence. Temporary work can be a way for job seekers to see what it is like to work at certain jobs or industries.

You can find staffing agencies in the telephone book and online. Check first to see if the agency places people in your occupation.

Usually, staffing firms charge companies a fee if one of the candidates they refer is hired. There is no cost to the job seeker.

There are companies that charge job seekers fees, which can run into the thousands of dollars. Thoroughly research the company before you sign any contracts or spend any money. Check your local consumer protection agency to see whether any complaints have been filed against the company. If you live in the United States or Canada, you can access the website of the Better Business Bureau (www.bbb.org). You can also do an internet search on "complaints against [company name]."

Contact Your College Career and Alumni Offices

Often, these offices provide assistance to their alumni well after graduation, although some charge fees after a certain number of years. Alumni networks can be valuable sources of networking contacts.

Attend Career Fairs

These events, sometimes referred to as career expositions (or expos), bring together job seekers and potential employers. Companies set up exhibits, which job seekers can visit to find out about openings, leave resumes, and speak with a company representative.

Career fairs are typically industry-specific, for example focused on employers in high technology or healthcare. They are often crowded and noisy. Attending career fairs is an unlikely strategy for people with Asperger's Syndrome. If you can tolerate the people and noise, these events provide practice greeting and interacting with employers, and might be a source of viable job leads.

Work as a Temp

As a job search strategy, temping provides current experience to include on your resume, and some income. If the employer likes your work, you could be offered a full-time, permanent job. This is also a way to check out a job or industry, without making a long-term commitment. People usually find these assignments through staffing firms that specialize in temporary placements.

Volunteer Strategically

Doing unpaid work related to your career ambition is another way to get current experience to add to your resume. If your ambition is to be a writer, then volunteer to contribute content for an organization's website or publications. If computer technology is your field, volunteer to assist with programming or other computer-related projects. The people you work with in the volunteer job might also be good networking contacts.

Volunteering is not limited to non-profit organizations. You can find local businesses that need help, or participate in a professional association.

Attend Networking Events

These are gatherings of professionals who work in the same industry or profession. Typically, they are sponsored by a business association. Attendees include business people looking for potential customers, professionals looking for new contacts, and job seekers. If you find the group format intimidating and overwhelming, consider "speed networking" events. These are very structured and involve a round-robin style of interaction. Each participant has two or three minutes to speak with another participant. After the time is up, everyone moves on to speak with someone else. Job seekers can summarize their background and ask for leads.

Make Direct Contact with Employers

Reaching out to companies, in anticipation of future openings, can be a very effective networking strategy. It will be discussed in detail later in this chapter.

WHAT NETWORKING IS AND WHY YOU SHOULDN'T FEAR IT

The value of networking is its efficiency. You connect with other people to share information, much like a computer network allows many users to share files. Every person you connect with knows other people, who in turn know people, and on and on. This chain of connections makes it much easier to get information. When I needed a meeting space for an eight-week program, I contacted four professionals in my network. In less than 24 hours, I was put in touch with the owner of a private practice. One email later, I had a space. *That's* efficient!

Notice that I described networking as the sharing of information. It is a reciprocal exchange. People are willing to contribute their time and resources in anticipation that you will return the favor if or when asked.

Networking capitalizes on the fact that people like to do business with people they know. There is a tacit endorsement when someone makes a referral. If I recommend a service provider to a client, *my* reputation is on the line. Therefore, I only make referrals to professionals I know.

Networking helps you to find a job more quickly and easily. A networking contact might:

- know of job openings at his company

- have contacts at a different organization that is hiring

- refer you to professionals with connections in your field

- offer advice that will make you more marketable

- share resources.

Many individuals with Asperger's Syndrome believe that they cannot network because they do not know many people. Others protest that their discomfort with interpersonal interaction precludes them from reaching out to strangers. However, networking skills can be learned, and a little networking can go a long way. If you conducted informational interviews as part of your career research, you have already done some networking.

THREE JOB NETWORKING STRATEGIES FOR THE NOT SO SOCIALLY SAVVY

There are three job search strategies that offer the benefits of networking without the distraction of groups. They are: one-on-one job networking, job seeker support groups, and online networking. Adding just one of these to your job search plan can significantly increase your chances of getting hired.

One-on-one Job Networking

This is when you connect, one-on-one, with someone who can assist with your job search.

The process of setting up and conducting a one-on-one job networking meeting is nearly identical to the one for informational interviewing. The difference is the context of the meeting. During an informational interview, you are learning more about an occupation. When you are job networking, you are looking for leads, referrals, and advice.

The natural starting point is to reach out to people you already know. These networks include your informal and formal contacts.

Informal contacts include: family members; friends; neighbors; acquaintances from your religious organization, volunteer activities or a hobby group; and community members you know, such as a real estate agent, healthcare provider, hairstylist, and the mailman.

Formal contacts include: former supervisors; current and former co-workers; college alumni and professors; athletics coaches; fellow members of professional associations; others with whom you have a professional versus personal relationship.

Make a list of the people in your informal and formal networks. After each person's name, write down how they might help. Like this:

Uncle Mike: engineer; has contacts at his company and other companies.

Brother-in-law Don: loves to socialize; knows lots of people.

Professor Smith: consults with engineering firms; knows department heads.

Susan Adams: works at ACME; met for an informational interview four months ago.

The next step is to contact each individual to let them know that you are looking for work and how they can assist you. Approach someone you know well using a conversational style. Here is an example that uses text from the section on informational interviewing in Chapter 3. There are minor changes, in italic, to reflect the different context.

> Hi, Uncle Jack. How are you and Aunt Rita? Everyone here is fine, and Dad says that he's going to call you next week about playing golf.
>
> *I am looking for a job as a meteorologist* in the renewable energy field. My interest is companies that are developing solar heating, solar thermal power, wind power, and hydroelectricity. Do you know anyone who might have contacts in the research and development departments of "green energy" companies, or at a municipal power plant? I'm eager to get advice from a director of research, staff meteorologist, or head of engineering.
>
> Thanks, Uncle Jack. I appreciate your help.
>
> Tim

This next example is a query to someone in your formal network, such as a former co-worker or college professor. The tone is more businesslike. Once again, this is the same text that was used for an informational interview query, modified for one-on-one job networking. The modifications are in italic.

> Dear Professor Harris:
>
> I hope that this note finds you well, and that you had a restful summer break.
>
> *I am looking for a job as a meteorologist* in the renewable energy field. My interest is companies that are developing solar heating, solar thermal power, wind power, and hydroelectricity. I'm eager to meet with research directors, staff meteorologists and engineering directors to get some advice about the "green energy" field *and where the best job opportunities are.* Can you direct me to anyone who could help?
>
> Thank you for your help, Professor Harris. *My resume is attached for your reference.* If you need additional information, call me at 617-555-5555.
>
> Sincerely,
>
> Tim Jones

Notice that even though your objective is to find a job, these queries are asking for *advice*. At first, this may seem counter-intuitive. However, the purpose of the networking is a discussion. If you approach someone and ask, "Do you know any companies that are hiring?" their response could be, "No." This ends the conversation quickly!

Ideally, people in your existing network will be able to refer you to their acquaintances. However, as with informational interviewing, you may need to go outside of your network as well. Plan who to contact based on job title and company. You might start with staff members of professional associations, or the executive director of a local Chamber of Commerce. Review the section on informational interviewing in Chapter 3, for instructions on how to find contacts, make inquiries, conduct meetings, and follow up.

Appropriate advice to request includes:

- where the best job opportunities are

- which companies are/might be hiring

- what skills should be emphasized to potential employers

- how to find out about new openings

- who else to contact.

You must present yourself as a capable professional. Do not imply that you are desperate, mention that you are about to lose unemployment benefits, or vent frustration that no one will hire you.

The biggest benefit of one-on-one job networking is that you are interacting with one person, in a controlled setting. You can prepare in advance and avoid the pressure of crowded networking gatherings.

DIRECT CONTACT WITH A COMPANY

This is a variation of one-on-one job networking where you contact a company you want to work for, in anticipation of a future opening.

All organizations experience employee turnover. People find jobs at other companies, are promoted or transferred, or company growth or restructuring create the need for new hires.

Many hiring managers make it a point to network with individuals who might be able to fill a future need. (Reminder: a hiring manager is the person who would make the decision to hire you. For example, a marketing director would function as the hiring manager to fill an opening for a copywriter.) They do keep resumes on file. By initiating contact, even though no job is currently open, you identify yourself as a future candidate. A hiring manager might even forward your resume to other department heads in the company, "just in case."

Start by identifying the specific companies at which you would like to work. Try to find between 10 and 20 companies. Using the techniques described in the section on informational interviewing, identify the individual who has the *function* of hiring manager.

Then, send the hiring manager a letter of introduction, along with a copy of your resume. Explain why you are interested in this particular company. Make the reasons appropriate to the company's interests, not yours. These reasons could be:

- you like or use the company's products or services

- the company is young and growing (and you enjoy the challenges of a start-up)

- the company is the leader in its field

- your work style matches the company's culture (e.g. innovation, quality, creativity)

- you appreciate the company's values, such as giving back to the community or "green" initiatives

- the company offers growth potential for its employees.

Conclude your letter by asking for a brief meeting. Follow up with the individual as you would with any contact. Here is an example of a query letter.

May 8, 2012

Ms. Jane Smith
Development Director
Museum of Interesting Science
555 Maple Street
Anytown, CT 00022

Dear Ms. Smith:

I have participated in Museum of Interesting Science programs ever since I was a child, and strongly support your mission to make science accessible to children and adults. My family and I are eagerly anticipating the opening of the extreme weather exhibit. ❶

I want to introduce myself in anticipation that you may need an experienced marketing professional in the future.❷ For the past three years, I have produced promotional materials that were used to develop $5 million in sales. These include direct mail packages, social media campaigns, websites, advertisements, and newsletters. My work gets results because I focus on benefits to motivate prospects to buy.❸

Prior to working in marketing, I worked for two years as a reporter for the *Village News*. This required me to develop strong relationships with area business people. I leveraged these relationships to solicit donations for the paper's annual Walk for Food event. My contacts responded with more than $10,000 in cash and in-kind donations.❹

I am excited at the prospect of joining your team. I've enclosed my resume for your review. Can we arrange a brief meeting, so that I can introduce myself and explain more of what I can offer the Museum of Interesting Science?❺ I will call you next week to arrange a time to meet. If it's more convenient, you can reach me at 555-555-1212 or sbanks@isp.com.❻

Thank you, Ms. Smith, for your consideration.

Sincerely,

Susan Banks
10 Oak Street
Anytown, CT 00022

This is an effective letter because:

 Opening explains the job seeker's interest in working for the organization.

 Next paragraph states the reason for the communication.

 Brief summary of marketing experience includes results that were achieved.

❹ This job seeker does not have experience working for a non-profit. However, she mentions fundraising experience (and results) she gained while working at a newspaper. Since relationship-building is an important part of non-profit development, the job seeker emphasizes this skill.

5 Closing asks for a meeting.

6 Job seeker explains that she will follow up about a meeting, and offers her contact information in case the recipient wants to get in touch with her directly.

Job Seeker Support Groups

These groups are for people who are looking for work. Participants share leads, contacts, advice, and support. Meetings take place on a weekly, biweekly, or monthly basis. Each person gets one or two minutes to introduce themselves, describe their background, and say what type of job they are seeking.

Groups may be open to people seeking any type of employment, or specific to people in certain industries or occupations. An internet search should produce groups in your area (e.g. "Manhattan job networking group," or "New England job seeker support groups"). You can also check with your local unemployment office.

Regular meetings can help to keep you motivated. There are online groups for job seekers, however they do not offer the same benefits as in-person meetings. I encourage you to attend a group in your area. It is a chance to meet people in your locale, practice the exchange of pleasantries and small talk, and participate in a group.

If you join a job seeker support group, you will need to prepare an *elevator speech*, also known as an *elevator pitch* or *30-second commercial*.

HOW TO CREATE A 30-SECOND ELEVATOR SPEECH

An elevator speech is used in various networking situations. In the case of job networking, the purpose is to describe your skills, experience, and desired job. It is so named because it is brief—you can say it in about the time it would take to ride an elevator from the bottom to the top floor of a building. In practice, an elevator speech is usually 30 to 60 seconds, although at formal job networking events, participants may be given a minute or more to speak.

The basic format is:

• state your name

• summarize your experience and qualifications

- explain the type of job or help that you are looking for

- tell the other person how they can help (e.g. company contacts, job leads, advice).

Here is an example:

"My name is Kelly Smith. I am conscientious, detail oriented, and certified as a Microsoft® Office Specialist. My strengths include database management and advanced formatting of Word and PowerPoint documents. I'm looking for a full-time administrative assistant position at a company in the greater Lowell area. Does anyone know of companies that are hiring, or that might be hiring, in the near future?"

In just five sentences, this job seeker communicates her most relevant skills and qualifications, and lets listeners know how they can assist.

This is an example from someone who is more experienced:

"My name is George Andrews. I am a licensed electrician with eight years of industrial wiring experience. My specialty is troubleshooting complex systems and installing telephone and data wiring and security systems. I can also run pipe in any situation. I am looking for the names of facility managers at office buildings and hospitals in the Worcester area."

Once again, the job seeker clearly summarizes relevant experience and states what he needs.

Brevity is critical for an elevator speech. Use a timer to determine whether your speech is too long. Too much information confuses listeners. If someone wants more information from you, they will ask.

In informal settings, your speech will be shorter (about 10 to 15 seconds) and adjusted to fit the situational context. Suppose Kelly is getting her hair cut, and the stylist asks, "How are you?" This is an opportunity for Kelly to let the stylist know that she is looking for a job. Remember the core concept of networking: everyone knows other people!

Inside of a hair salon, a formal elevator speech would be out of place. Instead Kelly could say, "I'm fine. I finished my Microsoft Office Specialist certification, and now I'm looking for an administrative job. You don't happen to know of any openings, do you?" The conversational style matches the informal atmosphere of a salon.

By the way, if you are thinking that this kind of informal networking is a waste of time, you are probably missing opportunities. An acquaintance of mine found a very good job…through just this kind of conversation with her hairdresser!

Repeat your elevator speech out loud until you have it committed to memory. Practice using a conversational tone—you do not want to sound like a machine. An audio recording, made for *your ears only*, will allow you to assess the quality of your delivery. A reminder: don't be surprised if you find the sound of your own voice odd at first. Most people do, so listen to your recording two or three times just to get used to your voice. Then, focus on whether your speech is too quick, too soft, too loud, or just right. Are you speaking in a monotone? Do certain words or phrases sound awkward when they are spoken?

Online Networking

Social media platforms are increasingly popular networking venues for job seekers. LinkedIn (www.linkedin.com) is a well-established site for business networking. You can create and post a profile, and use the basic service, at no charge.

Employers routinely search LinkedIn to find job candidates. In this way, your profile serves as an online resume. Take the time to develop a professional profile that communicates your abilities. Make sure that your profile is free of typographical and grammatical errors.

There are many ways that you can use LinkedIn during your job search.

LINK WITH OTHER PEOPLE YOU KNOW AND SHARE CONTACTS

If you find a job posted online, one of your contacts might work at the company, or know someone who does. The individual might be able to introduce you to the hiring manager. If you have scheduled a job interview, one of your contacts may be able to give you information about the position or company.

SEARCH FOR A SPECIFIC INDIVIDUAL

This is useful if you have an interview and want to learn about the person's background.

SEARCH FOR A SPECIFIC COMPANY

You can find information about the organization, and see employees who have LinkedIn profiles. This can help you find contacts at particular firms for networking purposes.

PARTICIPATE IN GROUPS

There are thousands of special interest groups on LinkedIn. Joining groups related to your field enables you to participate in discussions, ask questions and make contacts.

SEARCH FOR JOBS

You can create searches and receive notices of openings that match your criteria.

Here is an example to illustrate some of the ways that a job seeker can utilize LinkedIn. This hypothetical scenario features Bob, who is looking for a copywriting job, and Mary, marketing director at Acme Widgets.

Bob visits a job board and sees an opening at Acme Widgets for a copywriter. He goes to LinkedIn and searches by company to find Acme Widgets. He sees that Mary is the marketing director (and almost certainly the person who will hire the copywriter). When he views her profile, he notices that he and Mary have several LinkedIn contacts in common.

Reading Mary's background, Bob learns that she started at Acme Widgets as a copywriter, and has been promoted three times. He also learns that her focus is new product launches, an area where Bob has experience. Mary volunteers at the Humane Society, and previously worked at the same company that Bob's father did. Bob makes a mental note: if we meet, I can ask about her volunteering, and ask whether she knew my father's boss.

Bob also notices that Mary belongs to several LinkedIn groups. He decides to join two that look relevant. Now, he has something else in common with Mary. If he joins a discussion and makes insightful remarks, she might notice him.

Bob knows Jack, one of the contacts he and Mary have in common, fairly well. Bob emails Jack from his personal account (not through LinkedIn), figuring that Jack checks personal emails more often. Bob and Jack arrange a telephone call to discuss the job opening at Acme Widgets. The next day, Jack sends Bob's resume to Mary.

Four days go by, without a response. Bob decides to call Mary as a follow up. Bob writes down a script. "Hello, Mary," it begins, "this is Bob Johnson. On Tuesday the 8th, Jack Jones emailed you a copy of my resume. My background looks like a good match for the copywriter opening. I want to check that you received my resume, and see if we can arrange an interview. My telephone number is 555-555-5555. You can email me at bjohnson@isp.com."

Bob practiced reading his script out loud, then dialed Mary's number. He received her voicemail and left a message. Later that day, Mary called him back and they arranged an interview.

The LinkedIn Learning Center provides more information about using this networking tool. You can also search articles online about using LinkedIn for a job search.

HOW TO CREATE A JOB SEARCH PLAN

Reaching goals involves consistent action over a reasonable period of time. Creating a weekly plan, with a specific schedule of job search activities, is essential for keeping yourself on track. Otherwise, you may discover, too late, that your days become filled with activities that leave little or no time for a job search.

Your plan must be manageable, and contain activities that you will actually perform. Writing down what you will do, and when, increases the chances of this happening. If you are not employed, you should plan on spending about four hours per day looking for work.

Ideally, your plan will include four to six different strategies, at least one of which involves networking. Experiment with different activities to see which get the best results. One change can make a big difference. Geoff wasn't getting results by sending out resumes. He registered with a staffing firm, and within a week had two interviews.

We will talk about motivation and how to create a detailed, step-by-step action plan in Chapter 9. For now, select some strategies from the Job Search Activities template that follows. The Weekly Job Search Plan template that follows can also be copied for use in developing your weekly schedule.

✓

JOB SEARCH ACTIVITIES

☐ Visit job boards and respond to posted openings.
Which ones?

_____

_____

☐ Post resume on job boards.
Which ones?

_____

_____

☐ Create a LinkedIn profile.

☐ Join relevant special interest groups on LinkedIn.

☐ Networking:

    ☐ Find contacts for informational/one-on-one job networking.

    ☐ Send queries.

    ☐ Follow up on queries.

    ☐ Plan for a meeting.

☐ Register with one to three staffing agencies.
Which ones?

_____

_____

☐ Contact college career services office.

☐ Contact college alumni office.

☐ Register for temporary assignments (staffing agency).

☐ Make direct contact with target companies.

✓

☐ Join a job seeker support group.

☐ Join a professional association.
  Which one(s)?

_____

_____

☐ Attend meetings.

☐ Attend a career fair.

☐ Explore strategic volunteering opportunities.

☐ Practice responses to interview questions.

☐ Other job search activities:

_____

_____

_____

_____

_____

✓

WEEKLY JOB SEARCH PLAN

Print a copy for each week.

For the week of (date): _____

Goals:

☐ Send at least _____ resumes.

☐ Make at least _____ follow-up telephone calls.

☐ Send at least _____ follow-up emails.

☐ Other goals:

_____

_____

_____

	Morning	*Evening*	*Action Items*
Monday			
Tuesday			
Wednesday			
Thursday			
Friday			
Saturday			
Sunday			

CHAPTER 7

INTERVIEWING

KNOWING WHAT TO SAY

Occasionally, I have a client who has no trouble interviewing. The majority are uncertain about what to expect, confused about how to prepare, and nervous about negotiating the meeting.

This is not surprising, since interviewing is a complex social event. From the Aspergian perspective, much about the process is a mystery. Why are you asked about previous jobs, when they are listed on your resume? Why does the interviewer want to know about projects that didn't work out? What is the point of saying that you want the job, if you're not sure? Where do you sit? What do you say when you leave? If your greatest weakness is procrastinating, why can't you say so?

For Jordan, the whole process was so intimidating that he got angry and refused to prepare in advance. However, his spontaneous approach resulted in not having answers to basic questions, such as why he wanted to work at the company. Dan refused to accept feedback about his responses to questions. "I will not lie!" he declared. Unfortunately, "truth" for Dan was describing himself as argumentative—not a quality that most employers want in an employee!

The neurotypical perspective on interviewing is different. Organizations invest a lot of time and money screening resumes, interviewing candidates, performing background checks, and speaking with references. If you are invited for an interview, it means that you have the required skills and experience. The purpose of the interviewing process is to see how you will apply those skills on the job, and whether you will fit in to the organization.

"Fitting in" is an abstract concept, yet a very important part of how job candidates are evaluated. The concept of fitting in can be frustrating for someone with Asperger's Syndrome. There is no set formula for how to do this. It is an intangible idea based on behaving in ways that cause other people to have "reasonable or good thoughts about us" (Winner and Crooke 2011, p.10). This is in contrast to the Aspergian focus on facts and information. From that perspective, interviewing should be a straightforward process of matching data about an applicant to specific job criteria. The person with the most matches gets hired.

Neurotypicals, however, place a high value on interpersonal relationships. Much of what happens during a job interview is designed to evaluate how well you are able to work with others. An organization comprises a group of people who are working toward a common goal. An employee may work independently on a project, but he does not work in isolation. Every job involves some type of interaction with others. It may be limited to co-workers within the company, or include contact with customers, vendors, or other outside professionals.

Companies do not want to hire individuals who are perceived as unfriendly, arrogant, unenthusiastic, poor listeners, resistant to the ideas of others, or just difficult. Such employees lower productivity within the company, and can damage its reputation with customers. When an employer contacts me about coaching an employee, the conversation almost invariably starts with, "His technical skills are excellent, but…" The "but" is related to interpersonal skills.

Outstanding technical skill or a very high IQ is usually secondary to effective interpersonal interaction. In a survey of the top skills and personal qualities that employers want, the ability to work on a team was number one, followed closely by strong verbal communication skills. Technical knowledge was ranked seventh (National Association of Colleges and Employers (NACE) 2011).

Preparing for interviews involves planning how to best communicate your skills, experience, and ability to work in a group. This is what neurotypicals do. As the final part of marketing yourself, interviewing requires that you present the benefits you bring in a convincing manner.

At this point, you may be concerned, like Dan, that this means that you have to lie, or pretend to be someone you are not. This is not true. What you need to do on an interview is demonstrate that you can contribute, *along with others*, to the goals of your particular department and the organization overall. This involves following directions, accepting feedback, solving problems, and getting along with different types of people. Even if the job you want requires innovation and creativity, you still need to communicate your ideas to others and work within parameters set by the company.

Dan's definition of argumentative was stating his opinions and discussing their merits, relative to the ideas of others. He shared several examples of lively exchanges in which he had engaged. The trouble was that an interviewer would not have the background knowledge to interpret arguing in this way. Within the context of a job interview, a person who described himself as argumentative would be perceived as quarrelsome, and resistant to following instructions.

"It sounds to me, Dan, like you are not afraid to say what you think, or engage in a debate with others," I said. "As long as you are respectful of co-workers and aren't continually challenging their ideas, these are not bad things in the workplace. But the word argumentative has a different connotation. It is associated with being quarrelsome and difficult."

Sometimes, I work with clients who find it unsettling to revise or edit the information they present about themselves. "What difference does it make if I admit that I'm not confident, as long as I can do the work?" asked Jennifer.

It makes a big difference. An employer would be concerned that an employee with low self-confidence might: be afraid to share their ideas, make poor decisions due to self-doubt, react defensively to feedback or criticism, be hesitant to take action or follow through on plans, or be slow to recover from a setback. A supervisor would wonder whether the employee would be too timid to take on additional responsibilities in the future.

It is true that Jennifer is able to manage her feelings of low self-confidence and perform job tasks successfully. It is also true that the purpose of an interview is to highlight one's skills and abilities. Within the context of a job interview, sharing that you have "low self-confidence" is counterproductive.

During an interview, you have a very short amount of time to make a positive impression and communicate your potential value to the employer. You must select relevant information from your background, and present it in a way that makes managers willing to hire you. This is not lying. It is prioritizing and editing, based on situational context.

NAVIGATING THE INTERVIEW

Interviewing is a time-consuming process. Companies may receive dozens, or even hundreds, of letters and resumes in response to a posted opening. It is not possible to speak with every applicant. The candidate pool is narrowed to a small group who seem like the best match for the position. This group will probably number 10 to 15 people.

Before arranging an in-person meeting, candidates are screened via telephone or video conference. The purpose is to narrow the pool even further. Although the exact number varies by company, in most cases, three to five people are selected for in-person interviews.

During a screening call, you should be prepared to summarize your background, explain why you are interested in working for this company, and be able to state a salary range, if necessary (salary negotiation is discussed later in this chapter). You may be asked additional questions.

Plan ahead. These calls can be scheduled, which gives you time to prepare. If you do not handle the screening well, you will not have the chance for a face-to-face interview. Keep a copy of your resume near the telephone or computer that you will use. Review the job post prior to the call, since it will give you clues about questions you are likely to be asked.

Remember Kevin in Chapter 1, who received a call at 11:00am and asked if he could call the interviewer back because he just woke up? By this point in the book, you know that Kevin's request made a poor first impression. His other options were to: say that now was not a good time, and schedule a call for a later date; or allow the call from an unfamiliar number to go to his voicemail.

An in-person interview begins as soon as you enter the company's reception area. It is standard in many organizations to ask the receptionist's opinion of job applicants. People have been removed from a candidate pool because they were rude or appeared sullen to the company's receptionist.

Your physical appearance and the way that you introduce yourself create an initial impression. This impression sets the tone for the rest of the interview. Announcing yourself, greeting the interviewer, and exchanging small talk are essential interviewing skills. They were covered extensively in Chapter 3 in the section on informational interviewing. Here are some reminders.

- Turn off your cell phone before you enter the premises. Do not chew gum or eat candy.

- Plan to arrive in the reception area 15 minutes before your scheduled meeting time. If you arrive very early, wait before going to the reception area. Arriving too early can signal poor time management, just as arriving late does. It can be interpreted as nervousness or wanting the job *too much*. There is a template at the end of this chapter to help you plan your travel to an interview.

- Smile and announce yourself to the receptionist, "Hello, I'm Tom Smith and I have an 11:00 appointment with Sara Jones." It is not customary to shake the receptionist's hand, but do so if offered.

- When you meet the interviewer, smile, make eye contact, shake hands, and extend your greeting, "Hello, I'm Tom Smith. It's nice to meet you." The interviewer may not be the person who escorts you from the reception area. If this is the case, greet this person in the same way that you would greet the interviewer.

- It is expected that you will engage in small talk on the way the interview location.

- Smiling is an essential part of greeting someone because it conveys friendliness and enthusiasm.

- If you are not directed where to sit in the interview office, select a chair near the desk or the interviewer, and be seated.

Once you are seated, the next phase of the interview has begun. It is a matching process. The interviewer is evaluating your:

- skills and experience

- interest in the company

- commitment to doing a good job

- future ambitions

- ability to fit with the predetermined hiring criteria.

At the same time, you have the opportunity to evaluate whether the job, the company and the manager are good fits for you. It is expected that you will ask questions about the job duties and the organization itself.

You may initially meet with someone from the human resources department. Part of their job is to screen applicants, based on criteria from the hiring manager. Even though they do not make the final decision, their feedback is influential in the hiring decision.

The next person you meet will likely be the hiring manager. (A reminder: hiring manager refers to the person who ultimately makes the decision to hire you, and is almost always the person you will report to. Marketing director is the hiring manager when recruiting a copywriter.)

After this first round, the candidate pool is narrowed, to perhaps three or four people. At later stages, you may meet with other members of the department you would work with daily, as well as individuals from other parts of the organization. Depending on the level of the job, you might also meet with members of the management team.

Since promising candidates may be asked to stay and meet with other people in the organization, you should always have extra copies of your resume with you.

Each visit you make to a company is one round of interviewing, regardless of how many people you meet. After the first round, the parties will share their impressions, and decide which candidates to invite back for a second round of interviews. If you make it to a third round, you are probably one of two candidates being considered for the job. The total number of interview rounds will vary. When the economy is slow and more people are looking for work, companies can take their time when evaluating candidates. I know of people who have been on five rounds of interviews and met 12 or more employees.

The larger the company, the more formal the interview process will be. Some companies include personality tests, simulations, and other pre-employment testing as part of the selection process. Personality tests can be problematic for a person with Asperger's Syndrome. Most employers screen for individuals who are friendly and extroverted—if your responses indicate that you prefer to be alone, don't like groups, and need a lot of supervision, you could be disqualified as a candidate. You can find information about these tests, and practice tests to take, on the internet.

Candidates may also be asked to complete short assignments to demonstrate their capabilities. For example, a copywriter might be given an advertisement to write; a marketing director might be asked to propose ideas for launching a new product.

PREPARING ANSWERS TO INTERVIEW QUESTIONS

Some people consider themselves passive participants at interviews. They show up at the appointed time, believing that their role is to field questions as best as they can. This is the wrong approach to take. Interviewing is an interactive process that involves a significant amount of preparation on the part of the job seeker.

I have had clients who are veterans of 20, 30 and even 40 job interviews, who do not receive job offers. This is a sign that they are not adequately communicating their abilities. Here are the common errors.

Long, Rambling Responses to Questions

Failure to summarize and prioritize information about your abilities can get in the way of effective interviewing. Sharing too many, or irrelevant, details makes it difficult for the interviewer to understand and remember your key qualifications. Going off on tangents makes you appear disorganized. In most cases, your reply to a question should consist of three to five sentences.

Very, Very Short Answers to Questions

Providing too little information is just as damaging as giving too much. Three and four word answers don't tell enough about what you can do. Worse, they make you appear disinterested in the position. Do not assume that an interviewer "knows," based on your previous work experience or education, why you are qualified for the job.

Being Unprepared

Arriving late, forgetting the name of the person you are meeting, and not having extra copies of your resume send the message that you are not prepared for the interview. So do incomplete responses to questions, lots of "umms" and "uhhs," and not having questions for the interviewer that demonstrate some knowledge of the company. If you don't care enough to prepare for an interview, the employer will wonder, how much will you care about your work as an employee?

Not Showing Enthusiasm

Notice that I didn't say *lack* of enthusiasm. If you feel enthusiastic on the inside, but do not show it on the outside, the interviewer will presume that you don't want the job. Not smiling, speaking in a monotone, looking away from the interviewer, and not expressly stating your interest will be read as indifference on your part.

Preparing what to say in response to anticipated questions takes planning and practice. Focus on what to say along with *how* you will say it. Displaying a relaxed smile, making direct eye contact, and leaning slightly forward toward the interviewer convey interest. The better you understand the tasks and responsibilities of the job, and how you are qualified to carry them out, the easier it will be to answer interview questions.

Prepare for interviews by taking the following steps:

Review your Preliminary Career Research and Notes from Informational Interviews

Verify your skills, as you did when you wrote your resume. What are the most important criteria for this occupation? How do you know that you meet them?

Research Typical Interview Questions for Your Occupation, and the Suggested Replies

An internet search such as, "typical interview questions for a [job title]" should return a number of online resources. You can easily find websites and books that discuss common questions and how to respond. Keep the number of websites and books you consult manageable to avoid information overload, and confusing and conflicting answers.

Re-read the Job Post

(You *did* keep a copy of it, didn't you?!) What are top criteria? How will you fulfill them? Why are you interested in working for *this* company?

Generally, your answer to a question should be between three to five sentences long, and make no more than three points. Whenever possible, give examples of *results* that you achieved rather than simply cataloging the tasks you performed. Explaining that you modified a payment processing system, and made it 15 percent more efficient, conveys a lot more about your abilities than simply stating that you reduced the number of steps from five to three. If you are entering the workforce, you can talk about projects and activities during your post-secondary schooling, internship experience, or volunteer work.

The most effective way that I have found to prepare for interviews is to focus on one to three anticipated questions at a time. First, I ask clients to do some reading to get ideas about how to answer. Then, we brainstorm ideas. I give my feedback based on my former experience as a hiring manager. The perspective I bring is how the answer would sound to a prospective employer.

Practicing with someone who understands the interviewing process, and who is neurotypical (after all, you are competing in a neurotypical workplace), will make it easier to edit information about your background. Interview preparation is not about copying answers that you read in a book or on a website; it is about prioritizing and organizing relevant data.

Once a client determines the points that he wants to make, I suggest that he write them down as bulleted phrases. If you memorize answers to questions word for word, you will sound mechanical and over-rehearsed. Practicing using bullet points means that your answers will be a little different each time, making it easier to maintain a conversational tone.

It is imperative that you practice saying your answers out loud. Thinking how you will say something is different from actually speaking the words. You should rehearse a response until you feel comfortable, can make your points without a lot of pauses or "umms," and finish it without referring to your notes.

It is very hard to judge how we look and sound to others. Making video recordings of your practice sessions reveals whether you are speaking clearly, and sending the right messages with your body language. Perfect Interview™ (www.perfectinterview.com) is an online tool that allows you to simulate a real-time interview. Videos feature interviewers who ask questions, at random, that you answer on the spot. You can use a webcam to record your response, and re-record it as often as you like. Your recordings can be sent to another person, such as a job coach or counselor, for additional feedback. Individuals can access this tool for a modest charge.

Role-playing with a professional is another way to practice. Ask for feedback on both the content and delivery of your answers.

I also suggest that you view some examples of interviewing techniques. These are easy to find on the internet. One of my favorite resources is produced by Denham Resources, an executive recruiting, office staffing, and human resources consulting firm, based in California. Denham Resources' YouTube channel features video clips with examples of "good," "bad," and "ugly" responses to interview questions. Captions describe what is positive or negative about the answers. The clips are entertaining and informative. You can view the videos at www.youtube.com/user/DenhamResources.

The biggest interviewing mistake I observe job candidates make is inadequate preparation and practice. Reviewing answers the night before an interview is not enough. Throughout your search, you should regularly practice answering questions, so that you sound polished and professional. The more you practice, the more confident you will become.

COMMON INTERVIEW QUESTIONS AND WHAT THEY MEAN

To answer a question well, you must understand what is being asked. This may not be readily apparent if you are a literal thinker. Josh was completely confused when he was asked, "Why should I hire you instead of the other candidates?" After thinking about it for a few seconds, he said, "I don't know how to answer that, because I haven't met the other candidates."

The interviewer knew that Josh had not met the other applicants. The intent of his question was for Josh to summarize why he believed that he was the best person for the job.

There are several types of interview questions. Some assess your abilities, depth of experience, and knowledge of a job function or an industry. Others are designed to tease out how well you work with others. Behavioral questions look at past actions as indicators of future performance. They typically begin with a statement like, "tell me about a time when," or, "give me an example of," or, "describe a project that..."

Here are common interview questions, and suggestions about how to answer them. Even if you are not asked all of these questions specifically, you can use the information to respond to similar inquiries about your background, hard skills and soft skills.

1. Tell Me About Yourself

Translation: Summarize your relevant skills and experience.

This question is often asked early in an interview. It is not an invitation to share your life story. A good answer summarizes, in five to six sentences, the skills and experience that make you a good fit for the job. Mention your most relevant general and job-specific skills, as well as personal characteristics that are important for the position. An accountant could summarize experience in basic accounting principles, discuss proficiency with computer spreadsheets, and give examples of accuracy and attention to detail.

A bit of humor, if you are comfortable using it, can relieve nervousness and get the interview off to a good start. Accountant Todd could say, "I'm a numbers geek!" But don't overdo the levity. One or two bits of humor per interview is enough. You want to project friendliness, not goofiness. You are not interviewing to be a company comedian.

Avoid long, rambling responses that contain irrelevant details: where you grew up, a list of classes you took to earn your degree, or your recent divorce. Don't mention achievements from high school and earlier, unless they are truly significant. Earning the designation of Eagle Scout, for example, requires personal characteristics that include persistence, leadership, and teamwork. These are valuable in any job.

2. Why Did You Choose This Field?

Translation: What excites you about this work or this industry?

A strong response highlights aptitudes and abilities that are related to the job in question. For example, "Engineering appeals to me because I enjoy applying mathematical principles to solve real-world problems. During college, I did a project…"

A weak response focuses on your personal preferences instead of what you can do for the employer, "I like computers," "There are lots of jobs," or, "It pays well."

3. What Are Your Greatest Strengths?

Translation: What makes you good at this work? (Be ready with three examples.)

It is not boastful to discuss your abilities and accomplishments at a job interview. This is your chance to describe knowledge and personal attributes that enable you to achieve results for the organization. Choose strong points that demonstrate your ability to perform the job well. An engineer might say, "I can form detailed pictures in my mind and see how design changes will impact product performance."

Empty, self-serving answers are those that offer no benefit to the employer, "I'm a fantastic writer," "I'm a genius at math," or, "I live to write code!"

4. What is Your Greatest Weakness?

Translation: Do you have insight into your limitations and have you learned from your mistakes?

This is a tricky question. *Everyone* has weaknesses of some kind, so saying that you don't have any is clearly not true. On the other hand, being too honest can disqualify you as a candidate. Think about a weakness that is also a strength, or a limitation that you have overcome. Aaron said, "I can be a perfectionist, however this has helped me in accounting because my work is accurate. *And*, it is always delivered on time." This answer works because accuracy is important in this line of work, and Aaron added a sentence to let the employer know that his thoroughness would not get in the way of meeting deadlines.

Unacceptable responses are those that communicate a *fatal flaw*. This refers to an attribute that makes you unqualified for the position. Describing yourself as introverted and a little shy at first would be a fatal flaw for a salesperson, who meets with new prospects. It would not be a fatal flaw for someone, like an accountant, who works mostly with information. Some answers are fatal flaws for any job. Fatal flaw answers include, "I'm not a team player," "My self-confidence is low," and, "I don't like taking the ideas or direction of others."

5. Describe Your Worst Boss

Translation: What type of manager have you disliked working with (and am *I* that type of manager)?

This question is not as simple as it may first sound. I'll begin with the wrong answer, since it is the one so many of my clients choose. Rob is a good example. I could hear his agitation as he began describing a former manager. "He wouldn't give me clear instructions, and then blamed me for everything that went wrong," Rob began. "Once I asked to take a Friday off before a holiday weekend. He was so mean, he said no, but then let one of the other associates take Friday off."

I'll bet that you, like Rob, have a story or two about an unreasonable, jerky boss. However, sharing these anecdotes at an interview makes *you* look bad. Blaming problems on someone else, or making negative judgments about a person's character, makes you sound like a complainer, and an employee who is difficult to work with. Companies do not want employees who are difficult. Avoid comments like, "He didn't listen to me," "She criticized my work," and, "He was disrespectful and yelled a lot."

When a hiring manager asks this question, he wants to know whether you will be comfortable with his management style. A manager who gives staff members a lot of autonomy would be concerned if you describe this style as difficult. Obviously, you cannot know a manager's preferences in advance. If your styles are different to the point of incompatibility, it really means the job is not the right fit, and it's unlikely that you're going to get hired.

The right response to this question focuses on professional (not personal) characteristics, and frames negatives as differences in preference or style. For example, "My last supervisor preferred group brainstorming sessions. This was a challenge sometimes because I like to think about a problem on my own, then present my ideas to the group. We worked it out so I could contribute my ideas the next day."

6. Where Do You Want To Be in Five Years?

Translation: What are your career ambitions?

This question does not refer to geography. The employer wants to know about your future goals. A strong answer describes a realistic career progression, and shows a willingness to take on more responsibility, "I'd like to be developing strategies for new product launches, in addition to managing the existing line." If you are entering the workforce, the question might be phrased as: "What are your expectations for this job?" In a similar way, your answer should suggest a future career path, "I think it will be a great opportunity to apply what I have learned about journalism, and learn how to be an outstanding reporter."

A weak response is saying that you want the supervisor's job, as this will be interpreted as arrogance. Another is offering an unrealistic goal, such as becoming president of the company. Also avoid responses that suggest a lack of drive or low interest in the field, "Doing the same job," or, "I'd love to become an actor!"

7. What Did You Like Best and Least About Your Last Job (or Your Current Job)?

Translation: Will you like *this* job?

This is another question designed to see whether there is a match between what you want and what the open job entails. Your "best" answer should relate specifically to job you're interviewing for. Your "least" answer should concern a minor part of the work. A salesperson might describe closing sales as what he liked best about his last job, and filling out paperwork what he liked least. This is a good answer because the primary responsibility of a salesperson is to bring in orders, not fill out paperwork. It is well known that good sales personnel dislike paperwork.

Sardonic attempts at humor, such as "lunch," "weekends," or, "pay day" are sure to backfire as answers to what you liked best. Avoid mentioning activities that were a minor part of the job, even if you especially enjoyed them. A marketing copywriter who says that he liked proofreading best would raise questions or concerns. Poor examples of what you liked least relate to working as part of a group, or suggest laziness, such as "teamwork," "making small talk," or, "working late."

8. How Would Co-workers/Your Last Boss Describe You?

Translation: What are you like to work with?

You can answer this question using actual comments or your guess about how co-workers would portray you. What the interviewer wants to know is how you work with other people. Think about your role in group projects. Are you reliable? Helpful? Do other people count on you to catch errors, remember facts, research information, or fix technical problems? Your response should contain two or three positive attributes that are related to the job, "I believe that my co-workers would describe me as conscientious and skilled at analyzing data," or, "My supervisor said, at my review, that I am a fast learner and very accurate."

A poor response would contain negative characteristics or irrelevant observations, "Bossy," "Too shy," "Late!," "Really nice," or, "Tall with blonde hair." Self-aggrandizing statements are not appropriate, since this question is about interpersonal interaction. Do not say things like, "The smartest person in the company," "The only person in that department who knew what he was doing," or, "Awesome at writing."

9. Why Do You Want to Leave Your Current/ Did You Leave Your Last Job?

Translation: Are their problems with your job performance I should know about?

One reason that employers ask about former positions is to get an idea of your job performance and future ambitions. Anticipate that you will be asked why you left each of your former positions. In reviewing your job history, an employer looks for patterns of behaviors. Being fired from several jobs will raise concerns about your performance. So will a number of short-term positions, or jobs with decreasing responsibility. The question we are discussing now concerns why you left, or want to leave, your current or most recent job.

People change jobs for many reasons. These include: wanting greater potential for advancement, new challenges, more responsibility, chance to apply skills in a new industry, and better cultural/environmental fit (e.g. "I'm looking for an established company"). There can also be practical considerations, such as wanting a shorter commute, moving to a different geographic region, or being laid off. Any of these explanations are appropriate ways to answer this question.

Other reasons that people look for new jobs include: conflicts with a supervisor, belief that they will be fired, dislike of the work or working conditions, boredom, being passed over for promotions, stress and wanting higher pay. Making statements such as "My boss is unreasonable," "They won't give me a promotion," or, "I'm tired of working late" suggests that there are aspects of *your* performance that are sub-par. Saying that you want more money implies that you will leave this job as soon as you can find a better offer. An employer will not hire candidates whom they believe will leave after a short time.

Sometimes the choice to leave a job is not voluntary. If you have been fired from a job, be honest about it. Keep the explanation brief, and explain what you learned from the experience. Do not bad mouth the company or blame your supervisor. Here are some examples of how to explain:

- "Administrative work isn't a good match for me, which is why I am looking for a position doing research. My research skills include…"

- "The job contained much more project management work than I thought, so it wasn't the right fit."

- "A new manager came in and wanted to bring in people with Level 3 Certification."

- "My supervisor and I agreed that the job was not right for me, and that it was best that I find something else. I'm excited about this position because…"

Employers can understand one or two missteps. A person can be fired because a new manager has different preferences regarding important skills, or because the tasks and responsibilities of a job change. It is sometimes possible to negotiate with an employer and treat the separation as being due to a restructuring.

However, if you have been fired more than twice, the issue is not how to answer interview questions. You need to make an honest assessment of what is going wrong. It may be that you are choosing jobs that emphasize your weaknesses. Finding a different line of work, even if it requires an investment in education or training, will be worth it in the long run. Perhaps you need to improve your interpersonal communication skills, or your ability to organize and manage time. If you see a pattern, find out what the real problem is so that you can take corrective action.

10. What Have You Been Doing Since Your Last Job/Graduation?

Translation: Explain the gap in your employment history.

Periods of extended unemployment do not necessarily jeopardize your chances of being hired. Explaining that you were laid off, moved to a different geographic region, had to care for a family member who was ill, raised children, went back to school, re-trained for a different line of work, or tried freelancing or consulting are reasonable responses. The current economic climate has made it more difficult, even for college graduates, to find work. Employers understand that it can take months to find an entry-level job.

If you have been looking for a year or more, the gap becomes harder to explain. Employers worry that your skills are out of date. They might wonder why you have been passed over, question your commitment to finding a job, or wonder why you haven't sought part-time employment. These perceptions might be unfounded, but they can impact your search. My suggestion is that anyone who has been looking for more than six months should reevaluate their strategies.

Saying that you have done nothing, or have been "hanging out," is not an acceptable response for recent graduates. It suggests a serious lack of motivation.

As I mentioned in the first chapter of this book, doing some kind of work while you search for your desired job has many benefits. Whether paid or voluntary, it provides current experience for your resume and to discuss at interviews. It increases your confidence, provides structure to the week, and will keep you from becoming isolated and depressed. Engaging in some type of training that contributes to your skills or knowledge also provides a positive talking point at an interview.

11. Why Should I Hire You?

Translation: Summarize why you are the best person for the job.

Expect this question toward the end of the interview. It is your opportunity to summarize your qualifications and why you will do an excellent job. State, directly, that you want the job, even if you still want to think about it. Employers want to hire people who are enthusiastic.

A wrong response hints at desperation, "I really need a job," or, "I'll work for whatever you want to pay me." Do not make exaggerated statements like, "I'll work seven days a week," "No one else even comes close to matching my skills," or, "I'll stay here until I retire."

12. Why Do You Want To Work Here?

Translation: What is it that interests you about *this* company specifically?

I saved this question for last because it has tripped up so many of my clients. Whether it comes up during a telephone screening or in person, those who haven't prepared for the question often find themselves drawing a blank.

Your response should demonstrate interest and enthusiasm, in addition to knowledge of the company, "I share your commitment to making environmental issues accessible to the general public. The quality of your magazine articles and web content is excellent. I'm eager to contribute to your mission as a content developer."

Ineffective responses focus on what *you* want, "I've heard that you pay well," "The benefits are excellent," "I need a job," or, "I only live 10 minutes from here."

ANSWERING BEHAVIORAL INTERVIEW QUESTIONS

These questions are based on the premise that past actions are reliable indicators of future behavior. A common behavioral question is, "Tell me about a time when you had a conflict with a co-worker." If you respond by describing a loud, nasty exchange you had with an idiot who didn't know what he was talking about, the interviewer will assume that this is how you will handle conflicts at this company, too.

Behavioral questions focus on your ability to adapt to difficult situations, solve problems, learn from your mistakes, and get along with others. *The Career Coward's Guide™ to Interviewing* lists 25 different behavioral interview questions (Piotrowski 2007, pp.90–91). This might seem like an impossible number to answer…unless you know a couple of neurotypical tricks.

The first trick is to use the SAR method. SAR is an acronym that stands for Situation, Action, Result. You describe a situation, the action that you took, and the end result. In essence, you tell a mini story that illustrates how you reacted to a work-related event.

Paul was leading a five-day training course for new employees. On the second day, four additional people were added to the class, with no advance warning. Paul's problem was how to teach the new class members content from the day before, while keeping the rest of the class occupied.

Paul's action was to have the original class members read through the day two training material. He then explained the day one information to the additional employees. To save time, Paul used fewer examples and eliminated the group discussions. The result, Paul explained, was that everyone in the class was ready to learn the day two content after the lunch break.

"That sounds okay, Paul," I said, "but is there any result that would be more powerful?"

Paul thought for a few minutes. "Well," he said, "everyone had to take an exam at the end of the week, and they all passed."

"Great!" I said, "That is a quantifiable and desirable outcome, and will make a much stronger impression."

The second trick is to realize that one story can often be used in response to several different behavioral questions. In Paul's case, his SAR story is an example of performing under pressure, adapting to a difficult situation, finding a creative solution to a problem, surmounting an obstacle, and responding when things didn't go as planned. This doesn't mean that you would repeat the same example in response to different questions. What you will find is that as you go through a list of behavioral questions, one story will apply to several questions, making the preparation process manageable.

QUESTIONS TO ASK THE INTERVIEWER

Another question clients tell me they don't expect is being asked by an interviewer, "What questions do you have for me?"

This is a common query that you need to anticipate. Employers expect that you will want to learn more about the job and the company. Not asking anything makes you seem unprepared and disinterested. This is an opportunity to demonstrate your interest in the job, and learn further whether it is the right match.

Do not ask questions about salary, benefits, overtime, and vacation, until later rounds of the entire interview process, when you are close to an offer. Avoid asking very basic questions that can be answered by spending a minute or two on the company's website. Making such queries will be perceived as laziness.

Be ready with four or five questions related to the job responsibilities and the company. For example:

- What are the primary responsibilities of this position?

- What are the priorities for this position in the next three months?

- What is an average day like?

- How would you describe the ideal candidate?

- What does it take to be successful in this firm?

- What is the company culture like?

- Why is this position vacant?

- What opportunities are there for advancement?

- What is your time frame for filling the position?

Company-specific questions:

- I noticed that you've launched three new products this year; will that pace continue?

- Can you tell me more about the employee coaching program?

- How have the Article 3 regulations impacted this company?

HOW TO RESEARCH A COMPANY

The obvious place to start research is on the company's website. What are its products or services? Who are its customers? What is the company's history? Read through biographies of the management team. Are you meeting with one of them? Are there any positive observations you could make during an interview ("I noticed that three of your Vice Presidents won leadership awards")? Many companies post press releases, which can alert you to new products, noteworthy events, awards, and promotions.

Scanning the website of a local law firm, I discovered that it supported diversity and women's initiatives, and performed pro bono work for a children's charitable organization. The firm received a number of industry awards, and was voted Best Place to Work, for three years. One section described the firm's values and culture. Any of this information could be brought up during an interview, "I'm eager to know more about how you promote advancement for women," or, "I saw that the firm was voted best place to work three years in a row." If I was interviewing for a job in the marketing department, I could inquire about the recent awards for advertising and branding.

You can also get information by reading overviews in annual reports, or perusing white papers, or articles that are posted. One of my clients was able to discuss three articles she read that had been authored by the hiring manager who interviewed her.

The law firm had a page on LinkedIn. I clicked on the Insights tab, and saw several firms that people also viewed that might be competitors. This provided more information to bring up at an interview, "ACME Legal also has a real estate practice. Do you consider them to be a competitor?" I also noticed that I had connections to current and former employees. One of my connections might be able to introduce me to someone I could talk to about the firm.

My next stop was the social networking site Facebook. The law firm's page had links to articles by and about the firm, information concerning past and future speaking engagements and updates on various initiatives. If I was actively interviewing, or if this firm was one that I wanted to contact directly, I could "like" its page and "follow" the law firm on Facebook. If you were recruiting to fill an opening, wouldn't you be impressed by a candidate who could speak knowledgably about your company?

Other sources of company information include trade and professional associations, business sections of newspapers, standard business publications like Forbes, and specialized industry publications.

In most cases, you should focus on positive topics. Do not bring up a failed product, the senior vice president who was indicted, or the protesters at the last shareholder's meeting. Wendy was planning to ask whether people in the company were cliquish, as her friend had said. Remember, your objective is to express your interest in working at the organization and impress the people who interview you. Negative comments make a bad impression.

The exceptions to this would be if the company was emerging from bankruptcy, was being acquired, or if, for other reasons, you had concerns about its solvency. Once, during my marketing career, I joined a company that made a well-known misstep, and had brought in a new leadership team. I inquired about its financial condition and future plans, which included a large round of investor financing. It is also permissible to discuss negative events if you are interviewing for a management position that involves strategic planning.

CONCLUDING THE INTERVIEW

At the end of the interview, state directly that you are interested in the position. A number of my clients tell me that they do not do this. Even if you want to think about it, you should say that you want the job. The goal of an interview is a job offer. You always have the option of declining a position that is not a good match. However, if you appear disinterested during an interview, you will not get an offer.

Jack had many interviews over the course of seven months, but no job offers. He was qualified for the positions and answered questions well. "At the end of the interview, do you *say* that you want the job?" I asked. "No," replied Jack, stone faced. "Do you smile when you introduce yourself, and when you are leaving?" Jack admitted that it didn't occur to him to smile. My guess was that interviewers thought that Jack was not interested.

Jack practiced stating his interest, "This job sounds like an excellent match for my experience…" He also practiced smiling. Six weeks after making these two changes, he was offered a job.

After expressing your interest in the position, ask what the next steps are in the interviewing process. This will give you an idea of the company's process and time frame. The company may call applicants who are moving ahead to second interviews, or ask that you follow up at some point in the future. You might be asked to do a project to demonstrate your expertise. At various points in my marketing career, I was asked to write sample promotional copy, create a sample marketing plan, and suggest what marketing activities I would implement if I was hired.

Thank the interviewer for his time, and ask for a business card. Smile, shake hands, and leave.

I strongly suggest that you keep an interview log, with details about who you met, what was discussed, and future actions you will take. Update this document when you get home and the interview is fresh in your mind. There is an Interview Log template at the end of this chapter.

Within 24 hours of the interview, you should send a written thank you note via email or postal mail. Send a separate note to each person you met with. If you are sending postal letters, each individual's letter should be in its own envelope. Personalize each letter with something specific to the individual.

Remember, getting hired requires a marketing mindset. Use this letter to sell the employer on why you are the right person for the job. Restate your top qualifications, and describe the benefits that you will bring to the organization. Add additional details that you didn't mention during the interview. (But not too many; this letter should be no longer than one page.) Say that you want the job.

Here is a sample thank you letter following a job interview:

March 7, 2012

Mr. Paul Heymann, Chief Financial Officer
Lesner Enterprises
12 Main Street
Anytown, NY 14761

Dear Mr. Heymann:

It was a pleasure to meet with you regarding the audit trainee position. I appreciate the interest shown and the amount of time spent with me recently.

My college education and previous work experience shows that I will be an effective and productive auditor for Lesner Enterprises. Specifically, I match your criteria for an auditor who: will spend the hours, including nights and weekends, that are necessary to complete the audit assignment on time, is detail oriented and able to find all of the necessary financial transactions, knows which Generally Accepted Accounting Principles to apply to judge whether a transaction is valid, will work effectively with the accounting and audit staffs.

In addition, I have a demonstrated ability to utilize interviews and discussions to locate all of the necessary information—documented and undocumented—to ensure that needed financial data has been reported.

I am very interested in working for you and Lesner Enterprises. I am looking forward to another meeting and the chance to meet other members of the staff. I'll await your call at 555-555-5555. If it is more convenient you may email me at philipbrooks@isp.com.

Sincerely yours,

Philip A. Brooks
365 Maple Street
Mytown, NY 14762

Follow up with a telephone call to check the status of your candidacy. Call the hiring manager, not the human resources department. The general guideline is to wait seven business days following an email, and ten business days after sending postal mail. If the interviewer gave you a time frame for hearing back ("We'll decide which candidates are moving forward in two weeks") wait a day or two after the deadline before following up. Appearing *too* eager will turn off an employer.

You will repeat this process each time you conclude a round of interviews. Send notes to the individuals you met on *that* round.

SALARY NEGOTIATION

After seven months of searching, Alex was thrilled to have a second interview. Predictably, the topic of salary came up. "I said that I would work for whatever they wanted to pay me," Alex said. Mike graduated from a prestigious engineering program. He told me his desired salary. "That sounds very low," I said. "I know, but I really want a job!" Mike shot back.

Both Alex and Mike equated their salary negotiations with a retail sale. Offer a very low price, they thought, and the employer will buy. However, the way an employer looks at it, a person who is willing to work for substantially below the market rate must not be very good, has not done their research, or is desperate for a job. Employers don't want to hire workers who are mediocre or so in need that they will accept anything.

Benjamin was on the opposite end of this scale. He wanted a salary that was significantly above the market rate. He arrived at this number because he thought it was fair, based on the number of years that he had been in the industry. "I got a raise every year at my performance review," he explained.

This is not how companies decide wages. In Ben's industry, the economic downturn resulted in many people being laid off, including Ben! Fewer jobs, and more people looking for work, pushed salaries downward. Since organizations could acquire the skills they needed for less, there was no reason to pay Ben's inflated price.

Jobs that pay an hourly rate often have a specific range determined by the employer. Set increases are determined by length of service, output, or cost of living adjustments. There is not significant variation in the hourly rate paid to retail sales associates. In the United States and other industrialized countries, governments set certain minimum hourly rates of pay, and have laws regarding when employers must pay workers overtime.

Work that involves executing routine tasks usually pays by the hour. The upper and lower pay ranges are small because once tasks are learned, they are repeated again and again. No matter how skilled someone is at operating a cash register, there is a limit to what employers will pay a cashier.

Salaried positions pay a set amount that doesn't change based on the number of hours worked. Although people talk about a 40-hour workweek, in many salaried positions, it is expected that employees will put in the number of hours required to get the job done. In the United States, it is not unusual for business people to work 50 hours or more per week. When discussing pay for a salaried position, refer to gross annual salary. This is the amount before any deductions, such as income taxes. A computer programmer would state a salary requirement of $70,000 per year, not $1,346.15 per week. Commonly, the dollar figure is rounded to the nearest $500 or $1,000.

Many salaried positions have a fairly wide pay range. Average rates can vary depending on the complexity of the job, level of education or training that is required, years of experience needed, and level of responsibility. An organization may pay higher salaries for jobs that bring revenue into the organization, such as sales. Additional factors include the size of the company, the geographic region, industry norms, and the availability of qualified workers. People with very specialized expertise, or an established track record of outstanding results, are able to command higher salaries than the norm.

As a job seeker, you must know your realistic hourly wage or annual salary. It is useful to think in terms of a range. A small company, for instance, will not be able to pay the same salary as a major corporation. For some people, there are benefits that make up for less income. You might be willing to trade a smaller paycheck for a less pressured environment, the chance to take on more responsibility, fewer hours, less travel, etc.

When you think about compensation, remember to factor benefits into your calculation. Paid vacation and sick days, health insurance, tuition reimbursement, and retirement contributions are worth many thousands of dollars annually.

Think about where you would be willing to compromise. Would you be willing to take less than your ideal to break into an industry, earn steady income, have a short commute, or join a company that offered rapid advancement?

There are several ways to research average pay for your occupation and experience level. There are online tools, such as Monster.com's Salary Wizard®. Your preliminary career research should have yielded some information about salary range. Informational interviews are another source, although be sure to phrase your query as the range *you* could expect, not what the other person makes. Searching job boards by salary range is another way to gauge market rates. Networking contacts may also be able to help.

In most cases, if you are in a salaried position, you would state your desired salary in a range of $5,000 to $10,000. This could be more or less, depending on the job and your level of experience. Often (but not always) a spread of $15,000 or more suggests two different job levels. Careful research will enable you to decide on a realistic range.

Ideally, salary discussions should happen when the company is ready to offer you a job. Some interviewers ask for a salary range immediately, when they conduct a telephone screening. You can try to deflect this discussion by saying something like, "I'm willing to be flexible on salary for the right job." If the employer insists, you can say, "The jobs I've been looking at are in the range of $50,000–$55,000. Does that fit within your budget?"

At my last corporate job, I asked candidates for their salary range during the initial screening. My intention was not to find people who wanted the least amount of money. It was a small company, and I did not want to waste my or their time if we could not meet the person's requirements.

FINDING AND MANAGING REFERENCES

References are individuals who will recommend your candidacy to a potential employer. Usually, an employer will ask for the names of three people they can contact to discuss your previous or current employment, a college internship, or other relevant activities.

Speaking with references is another way that an employer verifies information and determines whether you are the right fit for the job. They may ask references about your performance, character, motivation, or how you handled certain situations. An employer may also verify to whom you reported, how many people you managed, or whether you were responsible for certain functions.

References can be a former supervisor, former or current co-workers, a mentor, the person who supervised your internship, a professor (if you are a recent graduate), someone with whom you volunteer, or a person you know through a business activity, such as a fellow member of a professional association. If you use co-workers as references, they should be your peers or above you in the organizational hierarchy, otherwise, the employer will wonder why no one at your level will provide a reference.

The human resources department can verify your dates of employment, salary, job title, and whether you left voluntarily, if you no longer work for the company. However, human resources managers cannot describe the quality of your work, so you should not rely on them as your primary reference. Many organizations make it a policy that human resources departments can only release factual information, due to legal concerns.

Inappropriate people to choose as references are family members, personal friends, medical or other personal service providers, and someone from your distant past (e.g. college sports coach if you are 40 years old).

Establish your references *before* you begin interviewing. Select individuals who can talk knowledgably about your qualifications, character, and accomplishments. *Always* get permission from the individual, and do not assume that he will agree. I have acquaintances who described their surprise when they were contacted as a reference for someone they did not feel comfortable recommending. This creates a very awkward situation for you, the individual, and the employer.

Even though your goal is three references, make a list of five people to contact, as one or two may not be available or willing. Call or email each person individually to ask for permission. If they agree, verify their telephone numbers and email addresses. Ask whether an employer can contact them during working hours.

Sample Script for an Informal Contact (someone you know well)

Hello, Geoff, it's Randy. I hope you are well and that you are still busy at work. I've begun looking for web development positions at high technology companies. I'm wondering if you are willing to provide a positive reference for me, based on the work we did together at ACME Software.

Let me know if you want more details about the jobs I'm applying for.

Sample Script for a Formal Contact (former supervisor, colleague you don't socialize with, professor)

Hello, Geoff, this is Randy Smith. It's been a while since we worked together at ACME Software. I hope that the job is going well for you.

I have started looking for web development positions, and am targeting high technology companies like ACME. I'm wondering if I can use you as a reference, particularly since you are so familiar with my design and implementation skills.

Are you willing to talk to an employer on my behalf? If you want to discuss my job search further, feel free to call me at 978-555-1212.

You also need a plan for managing your references. This means planning a strategy of what they will say to a prospective employer. Putting references on your resume makes this difficult to do, and I do not recommend it. Wait until you are at the offer stage and the employer asks for references.

Let the individual know when you give his name to an employer, and arrange a telephone call to discuss the job. This is important. You want to prepare your reference with details about who will be calling, the primary job responsibilities, aspects of your background that should be emphasized, and how they can address any concerns the employer may have. The employer will invariably ask references about what they perceive as your weaknesses. You want to know how the reference will answer this question, and if necessary, strategize the best answer with them. You do not want someone mentioning a weakness that could disqualify you from the job.

There is nothing dishonest about this type of planning. You are helping your reference choose information that is relevant to this particular job.

Ask your references to contact you after they have spoken with the employer. Find out what questions were asked and how the individual responded. If you discover that the employer raised a concern, you may have an opportunity to address it. For example, you could politely say, "Sue Jones, one of my references, mentioned that you were concerned about my ability to manage the full budget. I want to assure you that…"

Finally, let everyone who spoke with an employer know the outcome, even if you don't get the job. Thank them for their time and effort.

Letters of recommendation, which are endorsements from former employers or educators, may be shared during interviews. However, they do not take the place of live conversations with references.

IF YOU DON'T GET THE JOB

I know people who have been on four and five rounds of interviews, and do not get hired. It is very disappointing.

No matter how angry or sad you feel, be gracious. Express that you are disappointed, and wish the company success. Ask for feedback about whether there is anything that you can improve about your interviewing skills. The conversation might go something like this:

> "I'm sorry to hear that you offered the job to someone else. I hope the individual does well and that WidgetWorks continues to grow. I'm wondering if there is anything I can do better with interviewing." [Listen for response.] "Thank you. I appreciate the opportunity to meet you and learn more about WidgetWorks."

When this happened to me, I sent the hiring manager a note asking that she keep me in mind should there be a suitable opening in the future. Six months later, she called. The person they hired didn't work out, and she wondered whether I was still interested in the job. I was hired and spent several happy years at the company.

Do not act in ways that will alienate you from the people you meet during your job search. Managers change jobs and might be in a position to hire you at a different company, or recommend you for an opening.

There are many reasons that a hiring manager chooses one candidate over another. The new hire may have very specific experience, industry knowledge, job skills, or require less training. He may have been highly recommended by someone known to the hiring manager. The hiring manager could have a strong preference for certain characteristics, favoring individuals with MBAs, or those who appear very extroverted. The job seeker might be particularly good at selling himself. Sometimes the choice comes down to who seems like a better fit with the organization's culture, or with co-workers in the department.

There is not much that a job seeker can do about being turned down for a job. However, if you are repeatedly invited for interviews that end quickly, or never result in moving to the second round, troubleshooting is in order.

Clients who are having difficulty getting hired frequently admit that they did not prepare adequately for an interview. They didn't practice answering questions on a regular basis, and forgot what to say. Their research consisted of reading the home page of the company's website—and promptly forgetting the information. These individuals realize, after several unsuccessful experiences, that they need to devote more time to research, preparation, and practice.

I have also have clients who find implementing job search skills to be very challenging. They do fine when they are practicing at home or during a coaching session. But in "real-time" interviews, they forget what to say, become overwhelmed by a new environment, or become rattled when something unexpected happens.

If you have put in a serious effort and still have trouble, the best option might be to disclose your Asperger's Syndrome at an interview. In the next chapter, we'll discuss strategies for doing this, and how to decide whether it is right for you.

INTERVIEW CHECKLIST

Pre-planning

- ☐ Practice responses to anticipated interview questions.
- ☐ Research company; plan five or six questions to ask the interviewer.
- ☐ Research the person(s) I will meet with; prepare commonalities and talking points.
- ☐ Rehearse announcing myself to the receptionist.
- ☐ Practice greeting the interviewer.
- ☐ Create a portfolio of work samples (if applicable) of up to eight best examples.
- ☐ Select what to wear; clothing is neat and pressed; shoes are shined.
- ☐ Choose accessories (belt, jewelry, shoes, socks) that coordinate with clothing.
- ☐ Carry a portfolio or briefcase with extra copies of resume, pad and pen for notes, business cards.
- ☐ Allow time for personal hygiene on the day of the interview.
- ☐ Schedule haircut, if necessary, several days prior to the interview.
- ☐ Write down the interviewer's name, telephone number and address of the company and place it in portfolio or briefcase.

Transportation plan

a) My appointment is on [date]_____
   at [time] _____ am/pm.

b) In order to arrive at the reception desk 15 minutes before my appointment, I need to leave my home at [time] _____ am/pm.

(Note: if you are traveling during rush hour, or are not familiar with the area, schedule extra time.)

c) If I am using an automobile, I will park:

☐ in the company's parking lot.

☐ at a parking garage (location: _____ cost: _____).

☐ I have enough gasoline for the trip.

☐ I have money for a parking garage.

☐ I have money for tolls.

☐ I have printed driving directions.

☐ I am using a GPS system.

d) ☐ I have cash to cover incidental expenses.

e) ☐ If I am using public transportation, I have the bus/train/subway schedule.

✓

Readers have permission to download this template for personal use, from www.jkp.com/9781849059213/resources.

Contact Information	Action Taken and Date	Follow-up Action (what you will do, when, results)
Example: Carol Smith, Office Manager, Widgets, Inc., 300 Main Street, Boston, MA 02000. Tel: 617-555-5555; CSmith@ Widgets.com; www. widgets.com	9/15: Interview, re: admin assistant position	9/16: Emailed thank you note; 9/23: Called to follow-up; next interview on 9/27 w/ Carol and Anne Thompson, Div. Director

✓

Contact Information	Action Taken and Date	Follow-up Action (what you will do, when, results)

CHAPTER 8

DISCLOSURE AND ACCOMMODATIONS

ANTI-DISCRIMINATION LAWS

My clients frequently ask whether they should disclose their Asperger's Syndrome to a potential or current employer. I believe that the decision depends on the individual, their job performance, the specific challenges that they face, whether they have had a disciplinary action, and their comfort level with disclosing a disability.

If you live in a country that has anti-discrimination laws, such as the Americans with Disabilities Act (ADA), disclosing to an employer offers you certain protections. Some of my clients who were in danger of losing their jobs were able to receive accommodations that enabled them to meet performance expectations.

The risk of disclosing is that a job offer could be rescinded, a promotion denied, or employment lost, without the real reason being stated. Proving discrimination can be difficult, stressful, time consuming, and very expensive.

The ADA states that employers must provide equal opportunities to *qualified* individuals in hiring, firing, promotions, compensation, training and development, benefits, and other employment practices. A qualified individual is someone who meets the employer's requirements for education, skills, experience, and work performance.

This is an important point to understand. Employers do not have to lower their standards of quality or productivity for an employee who is disabled. Let's suppose that all customer service representatives are expected to enter a minimum of 30 orders per hour. Because of Asperger's Syndrome, your processing speed is slower; you can only enter 22 orders. You would be considered unqualified for the job.

Disclosing does not guarantee that you will receive a job offer or continue in your current employment. The law does not compel an employer to hire someone *because* he has a disability. It says that disabled individuals cannot be denied opportunities to obtain and maintain employment.

What an employer is compelled to do is make reasonable accommodations for qualified individuals with disabilities. An accommodation is a modification or adjustment that allows a person to participate in the interviewing process or to perform the essential functions of their job. The modification must be realistic and cannot cause an undue hardship for the employer.

The definition of what is reasonable depends on your job and the company. For Susan, a data entry clerk, requesting written instructions was reasonable. Ken, however, worked as a financial analyst. His supervisor explained that Ken's job required judgment. It was not possible to provide written instructions about how to address every possible situation.

An undue hardship at a company with 25 employees might not be considered an undue hardship at one with 10,000 employees. Modifications that would incur significant cost or disrupt an aspect of the business would be considered an undue hardship for the employer.

Here are examples of workplace accommodations that my clients have asked for and been granted:

- use of laptop for note-taking during meetings

- meeting notes taken by a colleague

- weekly meetings with a supervisor to clarify expectations and identify priorities

- written instructions for tasks and procedures

- lobby television turned off during the shift

- non-essential scheduling tasks reassigned to co-worker

- permission to take breaks when overly stressed

- requests from staff members submitted in writing

- interview questions submitted in advance

- switch to a technical job, from a management role

- move to a quiet workspace

- use of headphones to block out noise.

A further protection for employers is that an employee with a disability must be able to perform the essential functions of their job, or they can be fired. Essential job functions are the core tasks and responsibilities for which you are hired. For an accountant, using standard accounting software would be considered an essential function. If you have visual-spatial problems that make it impossible for you to use spreadsheets, you would be considered unqualified for the position. However, if you are a copywriter, entering budget information into spreadsheets once or twice a year may not be an essential function of your job. You can request an accommodation for tasks involving spreadsheets to be reassigned to someone else.

Employers do not have to accommodate employees who pose a direct threat to the health or safety of themselves or others, or those who engage in serious misconduct. Losing your temper at work can be considered a direct threat. Jack's work situation deteriorated over several months. He would frequently storm out of department meetings, muttering under his breath about procedures he didn't like. He exploded at one meeting, yelling at his co-workers about his Asperger's Syndrome and why it made it hard for him to interact with others. When his boss denied Jack's request to use vacation time, Jack sent him a threatening email. He was promptly fired.

You are under no legal obligation to disclose. If you choose to do so, your employer can request proof of your diagnosis from a qualified medical professional. They can also inquire about how, specifically, your disability impacts your job performance. Many companies have a form for your medical provider to fill out. You can, and should, control what information is given to an employer. It is not necessary, or desirable, to submit your full neuropsychological evaluation, or your entire medical history. Ask your medical professional to restrict comments to those items that affect your ability to perform your *current* job.

It is beyond the scope of this book to fully describe the Americans with Disabilities Act and the criteria for being considered disabled. Readers in the United States are encouraged to visit the website of the Job Accommodation Network (JAN; www.askjan.org) for a detailed discussion of anti-discrimination laws. JAN is a service of the U.S. Department of Labor's Office of Disability Employment Policy, and provides free information and consultations. Readers in other countries should consult the appropriate government agency. If you believe that you have experienced job discrimination, consult an employment law attorney.

HOW TO DISCLOSE IN A SOLUTION-FOCUSED WAY

In the United States, the ADA applies to all phases of employment, from submitting a resume or application to interviewing, to tasks and opportunities after you are hired.

If you decide to disclose, it is important that you do so in a solution-focused way. Most business people know little or nothing about Asperger's Syndrome. Making a general statement, such as, "I have Asperger's and can't multitask" puts the burden of figuring out an accommodation on the people who know the least about what you need to perform your job. Proactively suggesting solutions greatly increases the likelihood that your employer will implement them.

You must also consider the employer's perspective. Requesting accommodations is a process of negotiation. An employer does not have to comply with your request if it would cause an undue hardship, or interfere with productivity. A company is within its rights to offer an alternative accommodation that will address your need. Throughout this book, we have discussed the importance of working as part of a group, and managing the way that others perceive you. Accommodations should be requested, not demanded.

I have developed a three-step process for planning a disclosure strategy. The first step is determining *what* to disclose; the second is deciding *how* to disclose; and the third is choosing *when* to disclose. You can follow this same process whether you plan to disclose prior to being hired, or after you are on the job.

Step 1: Determine What to Disclose

Write down each challenge that you face, its impact, and the accommodations that you believe will solve the problem. Focus only on those challenges that impact you during the hiring process or on the job. Do not list difficulties related to your personal life or schooling. Here are examples.

Challenge: Processing answers to interview questions in real time.

Impact: Can't organize thoughts and communicate abilities.

Accommodation/s: Receive questions in advance of an interview.

*

Challenge: Learning new, multi-step processes quickly.

Impact: Overwhelmed by too much information; forget what needs to be done.

Accommodation/s: Break training into smaller segments; written notes.

Step 2: Plan How to Disclose

Your disclosure statement should be short, simple and to the point. Do not launch into a long explanation of the history of Asperger's Syndrome, theories about its cause, or all of the potential difficulties. Doing so will create confusion and raise questions about your ability to do the job. Trevor received a job offer and was concerned that his difficulties with social interaction might impact his performance. He drafted a two-page letter to the hiring manager that included quotations from the *Diagnostic and Statistical Manual of Mental Disorders*, which is used by clinicians to make diagnoses. Not only did his letter contain many details that were irrelevant to the workplace, it is highly unlikely that his future supervisor would understand terms like "restricted repetitive and stereotyped patterns of behavior" (American Psychiatric Association 2000, p.84). The letter also described "weird things" that Trevor did, including stimming, which he was able to control in public. Since he could control his hand flapping, there was no reason to discuss it. "Weird" is a poor word choice, because weird behavior makes people nervous.

When Lee disclosed she explained, "I have Asperger's Syndrome, a neurological condition that makes it hard for me to remember verbal instructions. During training, I need to watch how a task is done, make notes, and then practice the steps in order to learn them."

Step 3: Choose When to Disclose

Timing is the final aspect of a disclosure strategy. There are pros and cons to disclosing at various stages of the employment cycle. Once again, there are no absolute rules about when to disclose. It depends on your situation. Here are guidelines to consider.

DISCLOSING IN YOUR COVER LETTER OR WHEN SUBMITTING A JOB APPLICATION

Generally, I do not advise disclosing at this stage, because doing so puts the focus on potential problems rather than your qualifications. In many organizations, there is still apprehension about hiring people with disabilities. One concern is that the individual will require an inordinate amount of training or supervision. Another is that accommodations will cost a lot of money, even though according to a JAN study, more than half of accommodations cost nothing, and the rest cost $500 or less (Job Accommodation Network 2005–2001).

A third concern is that the company will be sued for discrimination, if an employee cannot meet performance requirements and is terminated.

However, if you need assistance submitting an application, or with the interview process, you must let the employer know beforehand. Ann had significant difficulty making eye contact, remembering to smile, and making any type of small talk. Trying to appear neurotypical on interviews caused her so much stress that she couldn't focus on answering the questions.

Ann disclosed her Asperger's Syndrome in the cover letter that she submitted with her resume. She had been referred to the hiring manager by the friend of a family member.

With Ann's permission, the friend mentioned to the hiring manager that Ann has Asperger's Syndrome. Ann's cover letter mentioned her disability briefly, and put it in a positive light. It read in part, "Please be assured that my disability will not interfere with my ability to do this job, and in some ways, will actually be an asset. I am very reliable, and am driven to do an extremely good job. I urge you to speak with my former supervisor…"

During the interview, Ann addressed her difficulties with making eye contact and remembering to smile by saying, "I don't show a lot of emotion because of the Asperger's Syndrome. However, I am very enthusiastic about this position and brought a summary of successful projects to discuss." The summary was a bulleted list of achievements in her past positions. It helped her remember points about her qualifications that she wanted to make during the interview. She was hired on a three-month trial basis.

Another reason to disclose Asperger's Syndrome at the application stage is when it offers a distinct advantage. If you are applying for a position with an autism association, for example, your personal understanding of Asperger's could be helpful in the development of programs or educational materials. Even so, Asperger's should not be the main focus of your cover letter and resume—skills and experience should be.

DISCLOSING DURING A JOB INTERVIEW

Generally, I do not advise disclosing at this stage, either. The purpose of an interview is to demonstrate your capabilities and explain how you can contribute to the company's success. Disclosure can get in the way of this by focusing attention on your limitations and on potential problems.

However, if your challenges are so noticeable that not offering an explanation will disqualify you from consideration, disclosure is a viable strategy. Slow processing speed meant that Allison needed several seconds to organize her thoughts before responding to questions. This could make Allison appear "spacey" and unprepared. She decided to tell employers, "Because of my Asperger's Syndrome, I need a few seconds to organize my thoughts in order to answer your questions."

DISCLOSING WHEN YOU RECEIVE A JOB OFFER

The purpose of disclosing is to request an accommodation. If you believe that you can meet the employer's performance expectations, there is no reason to disclose Asperger's Syndrome. You can always disclose after you are on the job, if you realize that you need a modification.

It is advisable to disclose if you know that you will need a significant accommodation immediately. In the United States, an employer cannot rescind a job offer because you disclose a disability.[1] An employer could understandably feel deceived if you wait until your first day to ask for a modification; it begins your working relationship in an atmosphere of distrust. Finding the right moment to disclose would also be awkward. The employer would be prepared to get you started on the job, not to modify your workspace or reassign non-essential tasks.

Dan's technical skills were outstanding, but he had a history of job loss, and wanted to try a new approach after his latest termination. He identified his problem areas and accommodation needs. Then, after receiving a verbal job offer, but before signing an employment agreement, Dan told his would-be manager that he has Asperger's Syndrome. He described how Asperger's affects his ability to understand body language and how he can sometimes appear

---

1. After an offer of employment is made, an employer *can* ask medical and disability-related questions, as long as they ask everyone who is offered the same kind of job. Once you start work, an employer cannot ask disability-related questions unless they are related to your job or are necessary in order for the employer to conduct business. If your supervisor notices that you are dizzy when you stand up, and your job requires you to operate machinery, for example, the employer has a reasonable belief that you have a disability or medical condition that could pose a risk to your safety and that of others and can ask questions about your health.

rude to people. He mentioned that he would need help with prioritizing and estimating how long a project should take to complete. It turned out that his supervisor had a family member on the autism spectrum. Dan was able to focus on learning the job, instead worrying about what to do first and by when.

DISCLOSING AFTER YOU HAVE STARTED WORK

This is the stage where most of the individuals I coach make a disclosure. Usually, the precipitating event is negative feedback from a supervisor, conflict with a co-worker, receiving a disciplinary action, being put on a Performance Improvement Plan (PIP), or having two week's notice to improve (which almost always means that you are going to be fired).

It might also be in your interest to disclose if: your work is consistently late or has to be redone, you receive feedback about the same performance problem three times or more, or you are confused about expectations, or cannot perform an aspect of the job.

The wrong time to disclose is in a moment of panic because you made a mistake or had an argument. Melissa nearly talked herself out of a job when she blurted out to a human resources manager that Asperger's Syndrome made it hard to remember faces, multitask and deal with interruptions: all basic skills for a receptionist!

DOS AND DON'TS OF DISCLOSING

Sometimes you can address workplace challenges without disclosing a disability. Developing a repertoire of explanatory statements may be enough to "neutralize" unexpected behaviors and smooth over misunderstandings. You could explain, "I'm hyper-sensitive to office noise and wearing headphones helps me concentrate," or, "I need to write the steps down in order to remember them," or, "I tend to be literal; let me know if I am missing the point." Asking to see a sample of what a completed project should look like, or to review priorities weekly with your supervisor, will not be seen as unusual requests in most cases.

If your requests are treated as preferences, and not taken seriously, formal disclosure may be necessary. Even if you have been treated badly, or blamed for a misunderstanding, approach disclosure in a professional manner. Dramatic proclamations that you have been abused, tortured, or persecuted can make you appear mentally unstable and immature. Threatening a lawsuit if your demands are not met puts the employer on the defensive, and very likely will result in a negative outcome. It is imperative that you speak to your supervisor and human resources representative when you are calm.

Be certain that what you need is an accommodation, and not a different type of job. Sean wanted to retain me to speak with his employer about accommodations. He worked in a warehouse and had received a written warning about his performance. He frequently forgot one or two steps in the process of sorting and moving shipments. He was also not keeping pace with the other workers. As we discussed the situation in more detail, Sean said that the noise and activity in warehouse were very distracting. He described himself as "thorough and slow moving."

I asked Sean what accommodations he needed. He wanted to wear headphones during his shift, and to work at a slower pace. The headphones were a problem because Sean needed to hear when a forklift was behind him. Instructions were often called out to workers by the supervisor. Slowing his pace wasn't an option since everyone needed to work at the same speed to move materials efficiently.

It was apparent that the warehouse position was simply not a good match for Sean. He was unable to meet the requirement for speed, or to consistently follow verbal directions. He agreed that he needed to find another job that matched his abilities.

A disability is not an excuse for disruptive behavior. Matt was placed on a Performance Improvement Plan (PIP) for losing his temper and cursing at a co-worker. "I can't help it if Asperger's Syndrome makes me explosive," he said. I agreed that low frustration tolerance is a feature of Asperger's (Attwood 2007). However, Matt needed to control his temper in the office. One condition of his PIP was that he was to receive coaching to learn how to lower his stress level and manage frustration.

You must be willing to follow through, when you agree to change an unacceptable behavior. By the time Matt was placed on the PIP, there had been two other inappropriate outbursts. Matt's employer made it clear that he needed to change his actions, or he would lose his job.

Accompanying your disclosure with a brief article about Asperger's Syndrome can help to foster understanding. Do not expect an employer to read a book about the subject.

Finally, be sure to emphasize your expertise and abilities. There are a number of strengths associated with Asperger's Syndrome that are benefits in the right job. They include:

- attention to detail and sustained concentration
  benefits: ability to spot errors; accuracy; not distracted from the task at hand

- excellent long-term memory
  benefits: recall facts and details others have forgotten

- tolerance of repetition and routine
  benefits: perform the same tasks without getting bored or burned out

- strong logic and analytic skills
  benefits: ability to see patterns/draw connections in data; objective view of facts

- vast knowledge of specialized fields
  benefits: develop in-depth knowledge and expertise

- creative thinking
  benefits: different way of processing information can lead to novel solutions

- perseverance
  benefits: stick with a job until it is done

- honesty and loyalty
  benefits: not afraid to tell the truth; stay with an employer long term.

CHAPTER 9

CREATING AND SUSTAINING MOMENTUM

GETTING AND STAYING MOTIVATED

You now know that finding the job you want is a *lot* of work. It is almost always a long-term process that involves months of effort before the payoff. A general rule of thumb is: one month of looking per $10,000 of salary. If you are looking for a job that pays $50,000 per year, it will take about five months to get hired. Although it is a general estimate, I have found this statistic to be accurate.

Many individuals with Asperger's Syndrome tell me that they have difficulty motivating themselves to follow through on activities that do not interest them. In *Developing Talents, Careers for Individuals with Asperger Syndrome and High-Functioning Autism*, Temple Grandin repeatedly encourages using an individual's special interests as the impetus for action (Grandin and Duffy 2004).

To be successful, you need to create a plan and sustain the motivation to take action over the course of many months. This process is described in terms of hill, skill, and will in *Executive Function in Education, From Theory to Practice* (Meltzer 2007, pp.87–88). First, you need to establish a clear goal (the "hill"), then acquire the skills needed to attain it, and then be willing to persevere until the goal is reached.

I notice several patterns in clients who have trouble maintaining momentum in their job search. Some become frustrated and give up when results are not immediate. It doesn't take long for a vicious cycle to establish itself. The individual doesn't see results and gets discouraged. Because he is discouraged, he doesn't take action. The lack of action leads to more lack of results.

The conscious avoidance of tasks that are not interesting may stop a person from putting in the amount of effort required. Some individuals are paralyzed with anxiety about one or more aspects of finding a job. Others become distracted, lose track of time, and realize that the day has been spent on everything except what was really important.

In *Asperger Syndrome and Employment, What People with Asperger Syndrome Really Want*, fear of change, the inability to recognize the consequences of not taking action, and difficulty making transitions are identified as additional barriers (Hendrickx 2009).

This chapter focuses on how to create and sustain a momentum throughout the job search. It may be the most important chapter of this book, because it is about action. Action is what gets results.

A BODY IN MOTION…

One solution to the inertia borne of low motivation is to simply force yourself to get started…on one thing…*now*! Many people discover that once they begin an activity, the actual doing is not that difficult. Action begets more action, and they are able to work longer and more productively than they initially thought possible.

To make a distasteful task less intimidating, set a timer for 15 minutes. Focus *only* on that task until the timer goes off. You will probably be surprised with your progress. A number of my clients report that once the timer goes off, they continue working in order to get the task completed.

One of my favorite strategies is the three-item to-do list described in *Find Your Focus Zone* (Palladino 2007, pp.144–145). Rather than fret over a long, overwhelming list of things that you need to accomplish, you select "the next three things to do." This is another focusing strategy. You concentrate on completing those three things. When they are done, you move on to the next three, and then the next three…

Establish a schedule, location, and routine for your job search. Having a specific area set up for job searching helps you maintain focus, and allows you to store materials, such as resumes, in one place where you can easily find them. I suggest that clients who are looking for work create a weekly plan. It includes set times each day that are devoted to looking for work, plus specific activities. This builds the discipline that is needed to have a successful job search.

Some people complete easy tasks first, because the sense of accomplishment motivates them to keep working, and then tackle more difficult projects. Others do the opposite: they finish demanding tasks first, when their energy level is higher, and then "relax" by doing easier ones (Palladino 2007). Experiment and see which way works best for you.

Being accountable to someone else is another way to sustain your motivation to get things done. This is one of the primary reasons that individual coaching is effective. You are much more likely to follow through on a commitment if another person knows about it (Canfield 2005). If you are not able to engage the services of a private coach, think about joining a job seeker support group, online support group, or set up a weekly review with a family member or friend.

Rewarding yourself with something meaningful is another time-honored motivator. Nancy de-cluttered her office in 15-minute intervals, three days per week. After each interval, she rewarded herself with 10 minutes of internet surfing time. Each time that Anne completes a chapter of her book, her reward is a bicycle ride.

BUILD YOUR CONFIDENCE

Most of my clients include confidence-building on their list of goals. One of the surest ways to increase your confidence is practice. I have clients who are so anxious about making a mistake, or so convinced that something new won't work, that they refuse to practice skills.

Set yourself up for success by achieving small wins. Many people become stuck trying to take one giant leap to change. They envision themselves going from their current situation to a new one, all at once. They begin thinking about all the different things they need to do, some of which they have no idea how to accomplish. They become overwhelmed and do nothing.

The solution is to break your goal into manageable steps and go for small wins. Instead of deciding to become proficient at interviewing, start with something more manageable. Practice responses to two interview questions, or how to greet an interviewer. Brief practice periods, on a frequent basis, are more effective than a single marathon session. Try practice sessions of 15 or 30 minutes, two or three times per day. Mastering small steps increases your confidence, which makes it easier to tackle bigger goals.

Striving for perfection kills motivation. "Perfect" is not attainable. Making mistakes is how you learn. If you want to attain mastery, you must be willing to goof up. If you make a mistake, put it into perspective. Messing up a job interview, although unpleasant, is not a catastrophe or failure.

The black-and-white, all-or-nothing thinking that is common among people with Asperger's Syndrome creates a tendency to give up too quickly. I have had clients describe events that happened years ago as evidence that things cannot change today. Their thinking is what is getting in the way. If you do not believe that a situation can get better, you will have little impetus to try something different or to take action. Be willing to change your perspective and try a new approach.

When you are pursuing a long-term goal, such as finding a job, set interim goals for yourself. This strategy builds on the sense of accomplishment to sustain your motivation and increase your confidence. Create three categories of goals: immediate (within the next two weeks), mid-term (within the next two to three months), and long-term (within six months or more). Immediate goals can be creating a 30-second elevator speech, or attending a job seeker support group meeting. Mid-term goals might be making a certain number of contacts by a specific date, or going on a particular number of interviews. A long-term goal could be finishing a class or getting a job offer.

SETTING AND ATTAINING GOALS

A successful job search requires a clear goal and a realistic plan for reaching it. You may be thinking, "Well, duh! I'm reading this book because my goal is employment, and I'm learning all of the steps!"

Yet "getting a job" is a non-specific goal. It is difficult to develop a clear strategy for reaching a goal like this. The objective is not well defined, there are no benchmarks, and there is no time frame. There is no way to tell whether other goals need to be reached first, such as acquiring job skills, or learning how to interview.

In other words, it's not a SMART goal.

SMART is an acronym that stands for Specific, Measurable, Achievable, Reasonable, and Time-oriented. There are five steps to creating a SMART goal.

1. Make the goal Specific.

2. Make success Measurable.

3. Select a goal that you can Achieve.

4. Check that your goal is Reasonable.

5. Make it Time-oriented.

Here is how Ben used this process to look for work in the accounting field.

Step 1: Specific goal: *Within six months, job as private accountant at mid- to large-size business that is within 30 miles of my home.* Target industries: *Healthcare, insurance, business consulting.*

Notice how this goal enables Ben to focus his job search based on type and size of company, geographic location, and time frame.

Step 2: Measurement of success: *Full-time, staff position.*

Step two defines how you will know that you have reached your goal. For Ben, it was being hired for a full-time position, not as a part-time, or temporary worker.

Step 3: Verify that goal is achievable: Ben has a degree in accounting, lives within commuting distance of employers in his target industries, has an up-to-date resume, good interviewing skills, and excellent references.

This step is a "reality check." Do you have the skills, ability, and resources to meet your objective? If you realize at this stage that you have set an unachievable goal, do not despair. You might need to take an intermediate step first, such as acquiring a skill. Or, you might need to adjust your goal so that it is achievable. Alicia realized that there were very few library jobs in her area. She changed her employment goal to archivist, a field with much greater demand.

Step 4: Goal is reasonable: Ben has the required education and experience, and is seeking a salary in line with what employers pay. The entry-level position matches his skill level. It is realistic to expect to be hired in six months. Ben is willing to devote several hours per day to looking for work, and has a plan that includes several different job search activities.

Steps three and four sound similar, but there is a difference. Step three verifies that you have set a goal that is possible to achieve. Step four verifies that it is realistic given your circumstances. For instance, while it is *possible* that you could find a job in one month, setting an employment goal of 30 days is not *realistic*. Unrealistic goals lead to frustration.

Step 5: Goal is time-oriented. Ben's goal is to be hired within six months.

Setting a (reasonable!) time frame for reaching a goal helps you to stay focused and motivated. Establishing an end date allows you to work backward and create a timeline for taking various actions. It also helps you to plan interim benchmarks to monitor your progress. Ben set an interim goal of having at least five interviews ten weeks into his search. This helped him plan what he needed to do to reach employers with a need for an entry-level accountant. If Ben reaches ten weeks with only one or two interviews, he needs to reevaluate his plan.

Monitoring your progress and adjusting your plan are integral to reaching goals (Meltzer 2007). If you notice that one strategy isn't working, do not continue it. Try something different instead. I remember speaking with a young man who had been job seeking for nearly three years. He was unwilling to do anything besides visit internet job boards. "I'm going to keep doing what I've been doing," he said, "and hope for the best." My guess is that he is still sitting at his computer, emailing resumes.

The SMART Goals Planner at the end of this chapter will help you to develop realistic goals.

FROM SMART GOAL TO ACTION PLAN

Once you have established a SMART goal, you are ready to develop and implement an action plan.

We discussed choosing job search strategies and developing a weekly plan in Chapter 6. This section describes how to break tasks into small, manageable action steps.

Most people find it easiest to create a weekly plan, with certain tasks scheduled for certain days, and perhaps, even certain times during the day. Your plan should be flexible enough for you to take advantage of unexpected opportunities. Sam was concerned about scheduling specific activities. "What if an employer calls me, and the only time they can schedule an interview is when I am scheduled to visit job boards?" he asked.

In this case, Sam would have to prioritize. He agreed that since an interview was the step before getting hired, it was a high priority activity, and would take precedence over looking for job openings.

Here is an example of how Wade made the task of networking with college alumni manageable, and scheduled it into his weekly action plan.

Action Item: Network with College Alumni

Monday

1. Write an email asking alumni for their assistance with job leads.

    a) Send draft of email to three friends for feedback (ask for response by Wednesday).

2. Get list of names from alumni office.

    a) Call school at 10:00am.

Thursday

1. Finalize email copy.

2. Email queries to ten alumni.

    a) Create a spreadsheet with each individual's contact information.

    b) Send emails between 8:30am and 9:30am.

    c) Schedule follow-up telephone calls for next Tuesday, 3:30–5:00pm.

Friday

1. Write a telephone script for follow-up calls (begin writing at 8:30am).

    a) Read script out loud until I feel comfortable.

    b) Tape record myself reading the script.

    c) Adjust script if necessary.

2. Make note to email next ten alumni on Monday morning.

You can use this method for each task in your action plan. This kind of step-by-step approach can turn "impossible" tasks into achievable ones.

Creating a basic template for yourself is easy. Begin by listing each of your goals for the week. Then write down the specific steps you need to take, and when you will do them. Like this:

Goals for this Week

1. _____

   Specific steps I will take toward this goal:

   a) _____

      when: _____

   b) _____

      when: _____

   c) _____

      when: _____

   d) _____

      when: _____

MANAGING ANXIETY

Everyone experiences anxiety. In the right amount, it can be a source of motivation. Concern about an upcoming interview can provide the impetus to practice responses to anticipated questions.

Anxiety is often a response to thoughts about what *might* happen in the future. This is different from fear, which is a reaction to an actual threatening event. Common triggers of anxiety include:

- performing a task for the first time (especially if the steps aren't clear)

- recalling a previous bad experience with the same or similar task/situation

- concern about making a mistake

- fear of being criticized or ridiculed by others.

Anxiety is a common feature among individuals with Asperger's Syndrome (Attwood 2007). For some, it becomes a chronic state. This is not surprising to me, since the world seems to be such a random and confusing place for Aspergians. Clients regularly express their exhaustion at trying to decode nonverbal communication, understand the intention behind someone's words, or figure out how to handle a situation.

I notice certain anxiety triggers that are common to my clients with Asperger's Syndrome. They include:

- not doing something perfectly

- speaking to people you don't know (in person or on the telephone)

- not knowing what to say

- anticipating a negative outcome

- being pressured to make quick decisions

- making decisions, in general

- changing circumstances or behaviors.

I have had clients who will not role-play interviews, because they are so nervous about making a mistake. (In this case, we brainstorm how a person could answer questions.) Others resist feedback because of their anxiety about doing something wrong.

Too much anxiety is counterproductive, and can be paralyzing. Coping with debilitating anxiety requires the services of a medical professional, and is beyond the scope of this book. However, there are techniques for managing mild to moderate anxiety that could get in the way of finding a job.

Josh was so overwhelmed at the prospect of interviewing that he would "wing it," and show up with little or no advance preparation. Each time, he would be asked questions that he didn't know how to answer. Josh left the interviews feeling disappointed in himself, and discouraged about finding work. After a few months, believing that he would never be hired, he made only cursory efforts to find work.

People often make assumptions about events in the present, based on their experiences in the past. If a past experience was negative, a person may presume that any future experience will be as well, no matter how much time has passed, or how much he has learned. Lynne struggled in a job that left her exhausted and with little time for anything else. Even though she had excellent skills and experience, she hesitated to look for something less stressful. Lynne said that the thought of looking for another job filled her with panic. "I can't interview," she declared. This statement was based on a bad experience she had over a decade before!

Two things that can significantly reduce anxiety levels are anticipation and preparation for events. Instead of assuming or guessing what might happen, you make thoughtful predictions about what is likely to happen, and prepare accordingly.

Josh and I reviewed what he knew about the purpose and process of interviewing. He bought a book about how to interview, and found reliable resources on the internet. The process started to seem more manageable.

The next step was preparation. Advance preparation increases your confidence, and helps you to feel more in control of a situation. Josh determined how he wanted to answer anticipated interview questions, and practiced his responses. At first, he said them aloud in his room. Then he and I practiced them during coaching sessions. Next, Josh made video recordings of himself so that he could see and hear how he appeared.

Over the course of a few weeks, Josh felt much more confident about interviewing, and restarted his job search in earnest. He was also realistic about his expectations. "I probably won't answer every question perfectly," he said, "but if I make a mistake, I'll say so and start again."

If you are in the habit of anticipating negative outcomes, try challenging them with the Possible, Probable, Unlikely test.

1. Write down the negative assumption.

2. Ask yourself, "Is it possible that this could happen?"

3. If the answer is yes, then ask, "How probable is it to occur?"

4. If the outcome is likely to happen, ask, "How can I prepare for a better outcome?"

5. If the outcome is unlikely to happen, ask, "What do I need to focus on instead?"

Here is how Diane used this tool to challenge her assumption about interviews.

1. Negative assumption: *I will say one wrong thing and not be offered the job.*

2. Is it possible that this could happen? *Yes, there is a possibility that I could misunderstand a question, or speak before thinking through my answer. It could turn off an employer.*

3. How probable is it to occur? *Fifty–fifty. I have been practicing my responses, and am more used to the process, so I'm not as nervous. I've learned about the wrong way to answer questions, and modified my responses as a result.*

4. How can I prepare for a better outcome? *Continue practicing as part of my weekly job search plan. If I'm asked a question that I didn't anticipate, request a minute to think about my answer, instead of saying the first thing that comes to mind.*

Reframing is another technique for reducing anxiety. In *The Psychology of Executive Coaching, Theory and Application*, reframing is described as "an alternative context." The author notes, "The way we feel is determined by the way that we look at things, how we ascribe meanings, and what we see as the context. It all depends on how we look at it" (Peltier 2001, p.132).

Many people with Asperger's Syndrome fall into the trap of black-and-white thinking. They see things in one way, and don't believe that there are other meanings or options. The reality is that you *can choose* to look at a situation in a more positive way. The thought that, "No one will hire me because I can't interview well" can be reframed as, "I improve my skills with each interview," or, "When I learn how to communicate my value to an employer, I'll be hired."

Reframing is *not* denying reality or making excuses. It is thinking logically about how to replace negative, self-defeating thoughts with ones that are positive *and that are also true*. A person with poor interviewing skills who thinks, "I'm going to ace the next interview!" is denying reality. A person who learns and practices his skills and thinks, "I'm getting closer to a job each time" is reframing.

MORE ANXIETY MANAGEMENT STRATEGIES

Learning to ride the wave of anxiety is another way to manage its impact. Anxious episodes come in waves. The feeling of unease builds and eventually reaches a peak, then lessens and fades away. Realizing that just when the anxiety feels the most intense, it is beginning to pass, makes it easier to cope.

Using positive self-talk can help you restore emotional calm and find solutions to problems. This is *intra*personal communication, or statements that you say silently to yourself. When it is deliberate and encouraging, self-talk can lessen anxiety and help you take constructive action toward your goals.

One of Karen's big challenges was managing time. "When there's a deadline, my mind freezes," she said. "I tell myself to just forget it, the task won't get done on time." Not very encouraging thoughts! Together, we brainstormed how Karen could talk herself through situations where there were deadlines.

Karen started telling herself, "You have plenty of time," and, "focus on just one thing now."

It takes time and practice to make positive self-talk automatic. My clients have reminded themselves by placing sticky notes in strategic locations, and leaving themselves voicemail messages. Karen kept her statements in a purple folder under her computer keyboard. "Every day when I see that folder, it reminds me to calm down and think instead of panic," she says.

Here are some examples of positive self-talk for various situations.

- *Preparing for job interviews*: "I am fully qualified for this position," "I clearly communicate my abilities," "This job or something better."

- *Restoring emotional calm*: "I have handled situations like this before," "When I'm agitated like this, I need to take a break," "When I am calm, I will figure out what to do." (Slow, deep breathing also helps you relax.)

- *Talking through a problem*: "Where have I seen this before?", "The checklist reminds me of what the steps are," "I can revise last week's job search plan, instead of starting from scratch."

- *Setting goals and monitoring progress*: "If I focus on this task for 30 minutes, it will be almost done," "If I rush through the cover letter, it won't get results," "I want to visit the gym this afternoon, so I need to finish answering emails by 11:30am."

As we have discussed earlier in this chapter, if you are getting anxious and overwhelmed, break tasks into small, easy-to-manage steps. Concentrate on one step at a time. Then move on to the next.

✓

SMART GOALS PLANNER

SMART is an acronym for Specific, Measurable, Achievable, Reasonable, and Time-oriented. This model helps you to develop realistic goals and a step-by-step plan to reach them.

Step 1: Specific goal (What do you want, by when?):

_____

_____

_____

Step 2: Measure of success (How will you know when you've achieved the goal?):

_____

_____

Step 3: Achievable (Do you have the skills, ability and resources needed to meet your objective? If you answer "no," what skills/resources do you need to acquire? Do you need to modify your goal?):

_____

_____

Step 4: Reality check: is the goal reasonable? (Are you willing to put in time and effort over a realistic time frame?):

_____

_____

Step 5: Time-oriented (When do you want to achieve your goal? Use this date to work backward and create an action step timeline):

_____

_____

✓

ANXIETY MANAGEMENT WORKSHEET

Describe a situation related to your job search that you feel anxious about:

_____

_____

_____

1. How important is the situation/activity to your goal of employment?

   ☐ Critical

   ☐ Very important

   ☐ Somewhat important

   ☐ Not very important

2. What is the worst thing that you can imagine happening?

   _____

   _____

3. How likely is it that the worst would happen?

   ☐ Extremely likely

   ☐ Likely

   ☐ Somewhat likely

   ☐ Not very likely

4. If the worst did happen, then what?

   _____

   _____

5. What can you plan to do next?

_____

_____

6. What do you already know about this situation?

_____

_____

7. What additional information do you need to prepare? Where can you find the information?

_____

_____

8. How have you handled a similar situation in the past?

_____

_____

9. What advice do you have for someone facing a similar situation?

_____

_____

10. How, specifically, will you prepare for the event?

_____

_____

11. What is a way to look at this situation (reframe it) so that it is less frightening?

_____

_____

CONCLUDING THOUGHTS

When I started coaching people with Asperger's Syndrome in 2006, there was little attention on adults, or employment. Those who had jobs had difficulty fitting in, and those without jobs had a very hard time getting hired. I knew a computer software engineer who was laid off by his employer of 20+ years. He was personally devastated.

He was hired at this job right from college. He had never had to conduct a job search, or write a resume. He had gone to many job counselors and personnel placement agencies. The demand for computer software engineers was strong. His family could not understand why he had trouble finding a job.

I knew why. He had Asperger's Syndrome, and even though he was very bright, he didn't know what to do. He couldn't call employers or send out letters and resumes because he didn't know what to say. When he did go on the rare interview, he couldn't answer why he was looking for a job, without providing a detailed description of his previous employment and saying how much he missed his old company.

He had few resources available then that knew about Asperger's Syndrome and even fewer that addressed employment. Six years later, both the general public and the business community are more aware of Asperger's. There is a genuine concern among families, professionals, and government agencies about the waves of young people on the autism spectrum who are coming of working age. An article in *The New York Times* estimates that there will be more than 200,000 in the United States alone, over the next five years (Harmon 2011).

In response to statistics like this, some innovative organizations are creating employment opportunities that utilize the strengths of autistic individuals. Specialisterne broke ground in this area in 2004. Founded in Denmark by Thorkil Sonne, whose son has Asperger's Syndrome, Specialisterne specifically hires people on the autism spectrum to provide outsourced IT services to companies. Specialisterne (http://specialisterne.com) is expanding throughout the world and recently opened an office in the United States. Aspiritech, based in Illinios (www.aspiritech.org), and the nonPariel Institute, in Texas (www. npitx.org), have adapted the Specialisterne model.

As valuable as these programs are, they do not serve the needs of everyone with Asperger's Syndrome. For individuals who are seeking jobs in the general workforce, the burden is on you to fit in with the neurotypical model.

Several months ago, I was speaking to a group of people with Asperger's Syndrome about job networking. I began by asking audience members about their concerns. Some of the answers were expected: anxiety about meeting new people, not knowing what to say, sensory overload from being in a room full of people. One man said that he thought asking other people for job leads or advice was unethical, because it provided an unfair advantage. He incorrectly associated networking with insider stock trading. Another man said, "I'm afraid I'll do something that other people think is weird." I thought of my software engineering friend and what he must have been thinking and feeling six years ago.

Reading this book cannot guarantee that you will find the type of employment you want. Doing the exercises at the end of chapters will make the job search process easier for you, but will not make it easy. You need to do the following things.

- Use the book as a guide, but it is your hard work and focused efforts that will get you hired.

- Review the appropriate chapter before you undertake a job search task, such as sending out a thank-you letter.

- Do not give up if your first efforts do not lead to a job offer or interview. The job search is a process that will take time.

- Follow the steps in each chapter. Setting up an informational interview is probably a new experience for you. The information provided will help you and you will be practicing your verbal and written skills at the same time.

- Record your results. Several times I mentioned keeping a spreadsheet or a log of your results. You can review the log periodically to help to determine what you are doing that is successful and not so successful.

  There is an old professional tennis saying, "Always change a losing game, never change a winning game." This is why you need to keep and review your results. If what you are doing is leading to positive outcomes, such as interviews, keep doing what you're doing. If you're having negative outcomes, the analysis of the results will help you determine why and what changes to make.

- Get out of the house frequently. Being by yourself is lonely and depressing. Just taking a walk around the block will energize you and improve your mood.

- Realize you are not alone. Get support from other people. Attend job networking meetings, talk with your parents, spouse, relatives, or friends about your job search efforts, and accept their feedback and encouragement. Reach out for professional guidance. Throughout the book, I have provided various resources that can help you—use them.

Thank you for reading my book. I hope it has been helpful to you. Best wishes for your job search success.

REFERENCES

American Psychiatric Association (2000) *Diagnostic and Statistical Manual of Mental Disorders* (DSM-IV-TR) (4th edition). Washington, DC: American Psychiatric Association.

Attwood, T. (2007) *The Complete Guide to Asperger's Syndrome*. London, UK: Jessica Kingsley Publishers.

Bureau of Labor Statistics, U.S. Department of Labor (2012–2013) *Occupational Outlook Handbook, 2012–13 Edition, Customer Service Representatives*. Available at www.bls.gov/ooh/office-and-administrative-support/customer-service-representatives.htm, accessed on 19 July 2012.

Canfield, J. (2005) *The Success Principles™ How to Get from Where You Are to Where You Want to Be*. New York, NY: HarperCollins Publishers.

Career Services at Virginia Tech (2005–2010) *How Employed Virginia Tech Grads Found Jobs After Undergraduate Degree*. Post-Graduation Report. Blacksburg, VA.

Cooper, B., Narendorf, S.C., Shattuck, P.T., Sterzing, P.R., Taylor, Julie L. and Wagner, M. (2012) "Postsecondary Education and Employment Among Youth With an Autism Spectrum Disorder." *Pediatrics 129,* 1042.

Farr, M. (2004) *The Very Quick Job Search, Get a Better Job in Half the Time!* (3rd edition). Indianapolis, IN: JIST Works, an imprint of JIST Publishing, Inc.

Grandin, T. and Duffy, K. (2004) *Developing Talents, Careers for Individuals with Asperger Syndrome and High-Functioning Autism*. Shawnee Mission, KS: Autism Asperger Publishing Company.

Harmon, A. (2011) "Autism, Grown Up; Autistic and Seeking a Place in an Adult World." *The New York Times,* September 18, A1, New York edition.

Hayden, C. J. (2006) *Get Clients Now!™: A 28-Day Marketing Program for Professionals, Consultants and Coaches* (2nd edition). New York, NY: AMACOM division of the American Management Association.

Hendrickx, S. (2009) *Asperger Syndrome and Employment, What People with Asperger Syndrome Really Want*. London, UK: Jessica Kingsley Publishers.

Job Accommodation Network (Original 2005–2011) *Workplace Accommodations: Low Cost, High Impact*. Available at: http://AskJAN.org/media/LowCostHighImpact.doc, accessed on 19 July 2012.

Mehrabian, A. (1981) *Silent Messages: Implicit Communication of Emotions and Attitudes*. Belmont, CA: Wadsworth (currently being distributed by Albert Mehrabian, am@kaaj.com).

Meltzer, L. (ed.) (2007) *Executive Function in Education, From Theory to Practice*. New York, NY: The Guildford Press.

National Association of Colleges and Employers (2011) *Job Outlook 2012*. Bethlehem, PA: National Association of Colleges and Employers.

Palladino, L.J. (2007) *Find Your Focus Zone*. New York, NY: Free Press division of Simon and Schuster, Inc.

Peltier, B. (2001) *The Psychology of Executive Coaching, Theory and Application.* New York, NY: Taylor & Francis.

Piotrowski, K. (2007) *The Career Coward's Guide™ to Interviewing.* Indianapolis, IN: JIST Works, an imprint of JIST Publishing, Inc.

Piotrowski, K. (2009) *The Career Coward's Guide™ to Job Searching.* Indianapolis, IN: JIST Works, an imprint of JIST Publishing, Inc.

Winner, M.G. and Crooke, P. (2011) *Social Thinking at Work, Why Should I Care?* San Jose, CA: Think Social Publishing, Inc.

Young, K.S. and Travis, H.P. (2008) *Communicating Nonverbally, A Practical Guide to Presenting Yourself More Effectively.* Long Grove, IL: Waveland Press, Inc.

BIBLIOGRAPHY

Dubin, N. (2009) *Asperger Syndrome and Anxiety, A Guide to Successful Stress Management.* London, UK: Jessica Kingsley Publishers.

Eikleberry, C. (2007) *The Career Guide for Creative and Unconventional People* (3rd edition). New York, NY: Ten Speed Press, an imprint of the Crown Publishing Group, a division of Random House, Inc.

Fairley, S.G. and Stout, C.E. (2004) *Getting Started in Personal and Executive Coaching, How to Create a Thriving Coaching Practice.* Hoboken, NJ: John Wiley & Sons, Inc.

Farr, M. (2004) *The Very Quick Job Search, Get a Better Job in Half the Time!* (3rd edition). Indianapolis, IN: JIST Works, an imprint of JIST Publishing, Inc.

Fast, Y. and contributors (2004) *Employment for Individuals with Asperger Syndrome or Non-Verbal Learning Disability, Stories and Strategies.* London, UK: Jessica Kingsley Publishers.

Fleming, C.A. (2010) *It's the Way You Say It, Becoming Articulate, Well-Spoken and Clear.* Bloomington, IN: iUniverse.

Gaus, V.L. (2007) *Cognitive-Behavioral Therapy for Adult Asperger Syndrome.* New York, NY: The Guilford Press.

Grandin, T. and Duffy, K. (2004) *Developing Talents, Careers for Individuals with Asperger Syndrome and High-Functioning Autism.* Shawnee Mission, KS: Autism Asperger Publishing Company.

Kursmark, L.M. (2006) *Best Resumes for College Students and New Grads* (2nd edition). Indianapolis, IN: JIST Works, an imprint of JIST Publishing, Inc.

Meltzer, L. (ed.) (2007.) *Executive Function in Education, From Theory to Practice.* New York, NY: The Guildford Press.

Palladino, L.J. (2007) *Find Your Focus Zone.* New York, NY, Free Press, division of Simon and Schuster, Inc.

Piotrowski, K. (2007) *The Career Coward's Guide™ to Interviewing.* Indianapolis, IN: JIST Works, an imprint of JIST Publishing, Inc.

Piotrowski, K. (2009) *The Career Coward's Guide™ to Job Searching.* Indianapolis, IN: JIST Works, an imprint of JIST Publishing, Inc.

Straus, J. (2008) *The Blue Book of Grammar and Punctuation* (10th edition). San Francisco, CA: Jossey-Bass, A Wiley Imprint.

Winner, M.G. and Crooke, P. (2011) *Social Thinking at Work, Why Should I Care?* San Jose, CA: Think Social Publishing, Inc.

Young, K.S. and Travis, H.P. (2008) *Communicating Nonverbally, A Practical Guide to Presenting Yourself More Effectively.* Long Grove, IL: Waveland Press, Inc.

INDEX